Sea Kayaking

Sea Kayaking

Johan Loots

First published in 2000 by
New Holland Publishers Ltd
London • Cape Town • Sydney • Auckland

All inquiries should be addressed to:
Stackpole Books
5067 Ritter Road, Mechanicsburg, PA 17055.

2 4 6 8 10 9 7 5 3 1
First edition

ISBN 0-8117-2921-4

Library of Congress Cataloging-in-Publication
information is on file.

Publisher: Mariëlle Renssen
Editors: Romi Bryden, Samantha Hillary
Designers: Claire van Rhyn, Éloïse Moss
Illustrators: Danie Jansen van Vuuren, Anton Krugel

Consultants: Derek Hutchinson (UK)
Roy Dumble (New Zealand)

Reproduction by Hirt & Carter (Cape) Pty Ltd
Printed and bound in Singapore by Craft Print (Pte) Ltd

Although the information and practical advice offered in this
book is backed by the author's extensive experience, no book
is a substitute for experience, and the publishers accept no
responsibilty for any injury or inconvenience sustained by
any person using this book or the advice given in it.

Publisher's Note
It is very strongly advised that
kayakers wear helmets and PFDs
at all times, under all conditions,
while out on the water, although
photographs in this book don't
always indicate this.

Author's Acknowledgements
I am indebted to Dr Tammy Shefer for her editorial assistance, Tracy Sassen — former Ladies World Waveski Champion — for her demonstrations of kayaking manoeuvres, David Rogers for his outstanding photographs, and the editorial team at Struik New Holland Publishers, who excelled themselves. Most of all, I wish to thank my family for their support — and especially my parents,

Francois and Latella, whose wisdom let me follow the scent of the sea at a tender age.

The Publishers would like to thank Guy Musson for his constant readiness to give of his kayaking knowledge and experience; Andrew and Derrick Mills of Brian's Kayak Centre and Leon Franken of Coastal Kayak Trails for equipment used in photo shoots; and Prijon-GmbH for permission to publish photographs of their equipment.

Contents

Introduction

'Journeys germinate like seeds; they depend on the fertility of the mind they fall upon'

Gary & Joanie McGuffin

(from *Superior: Journeys on an Inland Sea*)

Sea kayaking as a recreational activity is steadily growing in popularity today as more people, surrounded by the trappings of technology in our modern cyberworld, follow the call to seek untamed environments and create opportunities to exercise outdoors.

The first kayaks were fabricated three millennia ago, by people living in the frozen wastes of the northern hemisphere: the Aleut, of southwest Alaska and the Aleutian islands in the Bering Sea, and the Inuit from North America and Greenland. Depending heavily on the sea as a source of food, they fashioned their early kayaks (meaning 'hunter's boat') from organic materials like whalebone and wood for the frames, over which sealskin was stretched.

The 20th century saw kayak design move full circle. Starting with finely constructed wood-frame and canvas crafts in the 1930s, designers tried various materials, including fibreglass shells in the 1950s, and moulded polythene, Kevlar and carbon fibre in the 1980s. Now, the latest, foldable kayaks with their aluminium frames take the kayak back to its roots — that is, skins over frames. It appears that the sea kayak's history has borne out the philosophical premise that the purpose of all journeys is to return to the source and know it better.

The canoe, designed primarily for river travel, has for many years permitted the interior exploration of continents. The 20th century has seen the rise of interest in the exploration of the world's coastlines in seaworthy kayaks, and some fascinating books have been written by pioneering sea kayakers.

In the 1930s, Scottish kayakers Alistair Dunnett and James Adam set off from Clydeside to paddle to the Hebrides via the west coast of Scotland. In *The Canoe Boys*, Dunnett gives his personal account of how the two adventurers used sea kayaks to explore the coastlines of these remote islands. The book has become an adventure travel classic.

In the 1970s, British kayaker Derek Hutchinson's pioneering expeditions, which included a crossing of the North Sea in 1975—76, did much to popularize this exciting sport worldwide.

Canadian Maria Coffey gives an entertaining account of the ambitious trip she made with her husband in her book *A Boat in our Baggage: Around the World with a Kayak*. Collapsible kayaks can be lugged onto trains, ferries and planes, so, using modes of transport that varied from buffalo carts to tractors, Maria and Dag Coffey were able to travel around the world with their folding kayak. They paddled around the Solomon Islands in the southwest Pacific, on the River Ganges in India, on Africa's Lake Malawi and down the Danube in central Europe.

above SUSPENDED UPON WATER, THE SEA KAYAKER RELISHES THE INFINITE PLEASURES OF FRESH AIR AND OPEN SPACES IN THIS MOST ECO-FRIENDLY OF CRAFTS.

right THE DISTANT HORIZON BECKONS THE WELL-PREPARED PADDLER IN A SEAWORTHY CRAFT. THESE CONTEMPORARY TRADITIONAL, OR SIT-IN, SEA KAYAKS MORE THAN MEET THE CHALLENGE.

Celebrated American travel writer Paul Theroux is also passionate about sea kayaking. His book, *Paddling the Happy Islands of Oceania*, relates how he used a folding kayak to explore these remote islands and meet their inhabitants. A different type of tale is told in G A Jooste's *Blue Sweat*, in which he describes an epic voyage made by fellow South Africans Brian van Zyl and Andrew Aubin, who paddled their double surf-ski, sleek racing cousin to the sea kayak, 3600km (2237 miles) around the southern tip of the African continent.

Sea kayaking shares many of its maneuvers and techniques — and much of its equipment — with that developed by river paddlers. But it has also evolved refinements of skill and design that pertain to sea kayaking alone. Traditionally, a sea kayak has a closed deck and a small cockpit. The modern sea kayak is designed to be very stable and comfortable to fit its main purpose, which is exploring and touring. Sea paddlers must be prepared to face differing sea conditions, intricate or rugged coastlines, and to handle a craft that is loaded with camping gear and provisions. The challenge for sea paddlers is not only to test uncharted waters but to have acquired the necessary skills to engage with the elements. This involves using the appropriate equipment, judging weather and sea conditions with accuracy, and having an understanding of navigation practices so that paddling is undertaken safely, and without harming paddlers, marine animals or the environment.

Although sea kayaks are specifically designed for paddling on the sea, they are also often used for trips on large bodies of inland water, such as Lake Malawi in Africa, or on large rivers. The same equipment and techniques are used. You may choose to explore remote coastlines, to paddle vast distances, or simply to enjoy a healthy recreational activity. It is up to the paddler to determine, perhaps with the aid of this guidebook, what sort of activity he or she would like to use the sea kayak for, and what type of kayak would be most suitable for that purpose.

The sport of sea kayaking is driven by a massive body of nautical know-how that is supported by a system of rules pertaining to nautical rules of the 'road' and safety regulations. The paddler who meets the challenge by fully informing him- or herself of those rules will gain the maximum benefit and enjoyment from this exciting activity.

We have learned that in this busy modern technological world, we must seek contentment from wherever we may find it, and for many of us that contentment lies in the natural world. Perhaps your search is just beginning and you are destined to continue the quest that began in the Greenland of old. In this spirit, you may acquire a sea kayak, equip it and learn the appropriate skills. Then you may lay out your charts, choose a destination and embark upon your journey. If this book can motivate you to take that journey, it will have fulfilled its mission.

above ORIGINALLY DESIGNED FOR HUNTING IN BOTH CALM AND ROUGH SEAS IN THE FROZEN WASTES OF THE FAR NORTHERN HEMISPHERE — WITNESS THIS PADDLER NEGOTIATING THE JAGGED REMNANTS OF THESE MELTING ICEBERGS — ANCIENT SEAWORTHY KAYAKS WERE A SYNTHESIS OF AESTHETIC APPEAL AND FUNCTIONALITY; THEIR EFFECTIVENESS DEPENDED AS MUCH ON THE SKILL OF THE KAYAK BUILDER AS ON THE STEALTH OF THE PADDLER.

left SEA KAYAKING IS A TREMENDOUSLY POPULAR SPORT TODAY, AND HAS BENEFITED GREATLY FROM THE ADVANCES OF TECHNOLOGY. ANIMAL SKINS STRETCHED OVER WOOD OR BONE FRAMES HAVE EVOLVED INTO TODAY'S MODERN DURABLE PLASTIC COMPOUNDS MOULDED OVER LIGHTWEIGHT ALUMINIUM FRAMES.

Choosing your Kayak

eschewing motorized craft, you have decided to take to the sea in a kayak. The kayak you choose should fit the purpose you have in mind for it. Are you kayaking for exercise, or for recreation? Or do you need a kayak to facilitate another hobby such as bird-watching, snorkelling or fishing? There is a vast range of kayak designs to choose from. This chapter covers what you need to know to choose the ideal kayak for your purposes.

Construction materials

Materials influence a kayak's performance and durability. When making your choice, consider the material's properties in terms of strength and lasting qualities. Ideally, it should fulfil your particular requirements in a kayak and be aesthetically pleasing.

Plastic Most plastic kayaks are made of polythene that is 'rotomoulded': plastic powder is introduced into a heated mould which rotates to distribute it evenly. Sheets of plastic may also be blow-moulded in a vacuum. Plastic has the advantage of being strong and resistant to impact and, although heavier, is cheaper than fibreglass or kevlar. Most plastic crafts are recyclable. However, plastic may require professional repair when damaged, and is not as durable in the long term as boats made from other materials. It can be sensitive to ultraviolet rays if not UV stabilized.

Plastic kayaks need to be carefully stored to prevent warping. They also tend to scratch more easily and become 'furry', which can affect the kayak's hydrodynamic efficiency.

Polycarbonate This alloy feels like stiff plastic, but is more resistant to sun damage. It comes in sheets which are vacuum-moulded into the hull and deck of the kayak. Polycarbonate's long-term durability is not yet proven, although it is known to be vulnerable to shattering and difficult to repair. On the plus side, it is cheaper than fibreglass and is recyclable.

Wood A rare find these days, wooden kayaks can be made from kits of bonded plywood or strips of wood laid over a structure which is then covered in fibreglass and epoxy. Wooden kayaks are hardy and easy to repair but they have a tendency to absorb water, swell, become heavier and eventually rot. Some well-made wooden kayaks may become collector's items if they have been properly preserved.

Fibreglass Composed of fibre-reinforced plastic (FRP), which comes as cloth laminated with resin, fibreglass kayaks are generally made in moulds in two pieces which are then bonded together. They are durable, resistant to sun damage and are long-lasting. Scratches do not affect performance, although fibreglass is prone to damage on direct impact. Fibreglass kayaks are lightweight, good-looking and functional, thanks to their glossy gelcoat finish. They can be susceptible to delamination and loss of gloss, and may be heavy if improperly laminated.

Kevlar The registered trade name of a strong fibre called aramid (aromatic polyamide), which is similar to fibreglass, Kevlar is used by manufacturers of fibreglass boats to reinforce vulnerable areas, as well as for complete kayaks. Kevlar kayaks have the advantages of fibreglass boats but are stronger and more durable. Kevlar is also lighter than fibreglass — a bonus when it comes to loading and unloading!

However, boats made of Kevlar are more expensive and harder to repair than their fibreglass equivalents. Also, Kevlar's strength is compromised by constant exposure to ultraviolet rays.

above SEA KAYAKS AT THE READY ON THE WATER'S EDGE.
right DOUBLE SEA KAYAKS MAKE FOR TWICE AS MUCH FUN AND SAFETY, BUT REQUIRE SYNCHRONIZATION AND CO-OPERATION BETWEEN PARTNERS. THESE PADDLERS ARE NOT WEARING PFD'S BECAUSE THEY ARE SNORKELLING, BUT PADDLERS SHOULD ALWAYS WEAR A PFD.

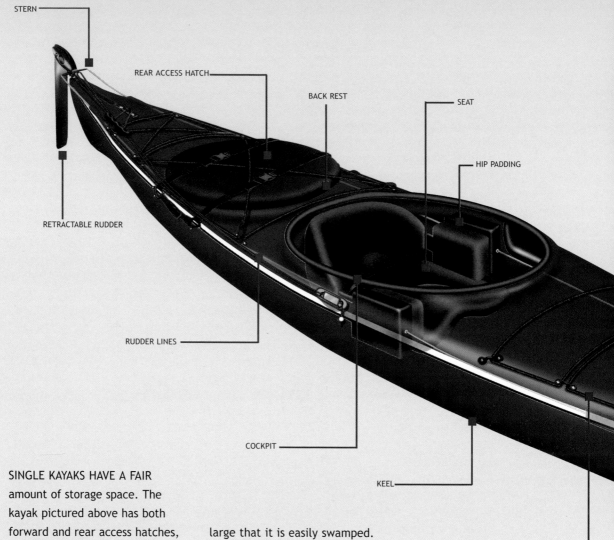

STERN

REAR ACCESS HATCH

BACK REST

SEAT

HIP PADDING

RETRACTABLE RUDDER

RUDDER LINES

COCKPIT

KEEL

DECK LINES

SINGLE KAYAKS HAVE A FAIR amount of storage space. The kayak pictured above has both forward and rear access hatches, and front storage space, allowing plenty of space for stowing equipment and gear. Items which need to be easily available, such as the spare paddle, can be stowed on deck, firmly secured with deck bungees.

The cockpit of your kayak needs to be large enough to accommodate you, but not so large that it is easily swamped. It is essential that you are comfortable and can manoeuvre easily. This kayak has a fitted back rest, which some people find eases back strain on long trips. The back rest should not ride too high above the deck level. Padding on the sides of the cockpit can make it more comfortable to lean the kayak.

Modern kayaks have come a long way from the original 'skin over wooden frame' kayaks used by the Aleut and the Inuit. The basic shape of the kayak remains the same, but variations in length, hull shape, rocker and weight can make a big difference to the performance of a kayak in experienced hands.

When choosing a kayak for yourself, remember that you are the one who will be paddling long distances in it, possibly with a heavy load. No matter what anyone tells you about a kayak's different attributes, you need to feel comfortable, even after a few hours of paddling. If you can, test—paddle a kayak before you buy it. At the very least, sit in the kayak to find out whether you fit comfortably in the cockpit.

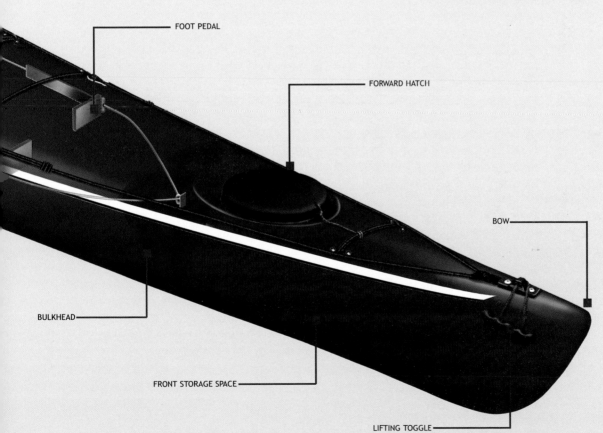

DECK BUNGEES

FOOT PEDAL

FORWARD HATCH

BOW

BULKHEAD

FRONT STORAGE SPACE

LIFTING TOGGLE

Classes of kayak

THE VARIOUS OPTIONS INCLUDE traditional (sit-in) kayaks, sit-on-tops, rigid hulls, folding boats, and single or double boats. To make your personal choice, weigh up the pros and cons of the various classes of kayak.

Traditional boats

The contemporary sea kayak market is dominated by rigid hull boats with 'sit-in' cockpits. There is diversity within this classification and each type has strengths and weaknesses.

Advantages

■ Designed for long distances and inclement weather
■ Protects the lower body from exposure
■ Combines manoeuvrability with tracking and speed

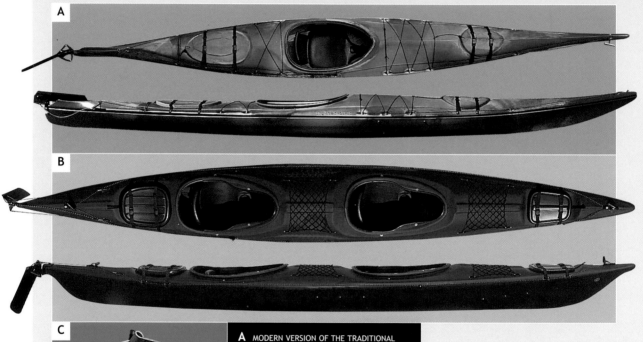

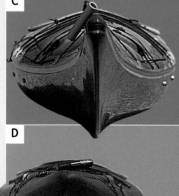

A MODERN VERSION OF THE TRADITIONAL SINGLE-SEATER 'SIT-IN' KAYAK WITH SEALED HATCHES, BULKHEADS, COCKPIT AND RUDDER SYSTEM. IT IS IDEALLY SUITED TO COOLER CLIMATES AND CALM SEAS, ALTHOUGH IN THE HANDS OF AN EXPERIENCED PADDLER IT CAN HANDLE ALMOST ANY CONDITIONS.
B A COMPACT DOUBLE 'SIT-IN' KAYAK WITH HATCHES FORE AND AFT. PADDLING TOGETHER HALVES THE EFFORT AND IS SAFER.
C SHALLOW 'V' HULL WHICH PROVIDES FOR A STABLE YET RESPONSIVE PERFORMANCE.
D DEEP V-SHAPED HULL LEADING TO A FLAT BOTTOM.

■ Built-in bulkheads provide flotation at bow and stern
■ Adequate storage space with hatches for easy access

Disadvantages

■ Launches and landings both require skill
■ Particular skills needed for self- and assisted rescues
■ Possible sense of confinement

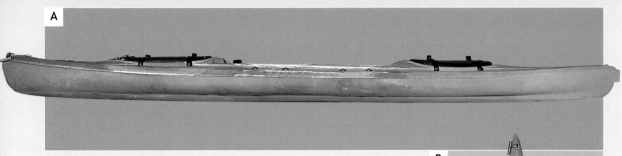

Sit-on boats

These have rigid hulls with moulded cockpit indentations. Sleeker hybrid versions, which combine the irrefutable qualities of sit-ons with those of successful 'sit-in' sea kayaks, may become the kayak of choice in the future.

Advantages

■ Easy to embark and disembark; it is also easier than the traditional design to remount after capsizing

■ Inherent buoyancy as a result of being a closed unit

■ Suitable for recreational paddling as well as tripping and touring

■ Handy for snorkelling and scuba diving; some models take strap-on containers and tanks

■ Rolling is unnecessary

Disadvantages

■ The kayaker is exposed to inclement weather and rough sea conditions

■ Looser fit makes it less responsive to paddling strokes such as draws and braces

■ Most sit-on kayaks currently available are best for day-trips, and may not be suitable for longer trips, mainly due to the paddler's constant exposure to sea and sun

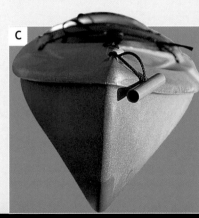

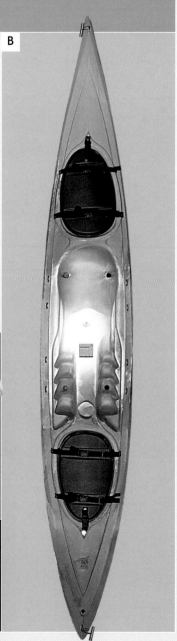

A and **B** POPULAR SIT-ON SEA KAYAKS WITH SEAT INDENTATION, SUBSTANTIAL HATCHES AND PROVISION FOR A RUDDER SYSTEM. SIT-ONS ARE IDEAL FOR WARMER CLIMATES AND SURF CONDITIONS, AND COMBINE WELL WITH OTHER ACTIVITIES SUCH AS DIVING AND FISHING.

C THE V-SHAPED HULL OF THIS SEA KAYAK IMPROVES ITS ABILITY TO SLICE THROUGH WATER AND ITS OVERALL PERFORMANCE.

Double and triple kayaks

More paddlers can mean more fun! Double and triple designs are available. Do try one out before embarking on a long trip as you, or your partners, may not enjoy the experience of having to work as a team. Bear in mind that some of the paddling and rescue techniques used differ from those for single kayaks.

Advantages

■ Beginners feel secure, thanks to the broader beam of the craft, and the companionship
■ Re-entry after capsize is easier as partners will help each other
■ Stronger paddlers can complement weaker ones

Disadvantages

■ Offers less storage than two singles
■ Greater weight is harder to manage, particularly loading and unloading from vehicles
■ Restricts paddlers to what can be achieved by the partner
■ Less manouevrable, harder to turn or surf
■ It is a challenge to find a double to suit both paddlers
■ Paddlers are restricted to availability of partners

Folding kayaks

Traditionally, folding kayaks were wooden frames with canvas and rubber hulls. Recent designs use aluminium and polyethylene for frames and Hypalon (nylon) replaces canvas.

Advantages

■ Lightweight and modern in design, but also aesthetically pleasing
■ Fold-up design for easy transportation and carrying
■ Durable, with replaceable 'skin'

left DOUBLE SEA KAYAKS MAY BE THE SAFER OPTION ON LONGER TRIPS; PFD'S, OF COURSE, SHOULD BE WORN, NOT LEFT ON DECK!
below SETTING UP A FOLD-UP KAYAK CLOSE TO THE WATER'S EDGE ELIMINATES DIFFICULT CARRYING.

Disadvantages

■ Assembly is time-consuming and takes skill
■ Flexibility reduces efficiency, requiring more effort to paddle
■ Lack of internal bulkheads reduces flotation, although most folding kayaks have inflatable sponsons (bladders inside or outside the hull)

Sectional kayaks

The sectional hard-shell kayak usually comes in three sections that bolt together. Each has its own bulkhead, making it stronger than a one-piece kayak.

Advantages

■ Flotation-wise has all the advantages of rigid hull kayaks
■ Easy to transport and store

Disadvantages

■ Not as easily portable as the folding sea kayak
■ Is heavier than either the fold-up or the rigid-hull-type sea kayak

Inflatables

Top-quality inflatable kayaks are made of tough materials like PVC or Hypalon which are able to withstand abrasive rocks and jagged coral reefs.

Advantages

■ Roll into small packages for easy transportation
■ Virtually unsinkable; even if punctured, their multiple chambers prevent the kayak from sinking

Disadvantages

■ Susceptible to puncture by sharp objects
■ Much more vulnerable to wind – they are easily blown over
■ Both paddler and gear are exposed to the elements
■ Keel not sufficiently rigid for long-distance travel
■ Inflation requires the carrying of an effective pump

left A SECTIONAL KAYAK (SHOWN DISASSEMBLED AND ASSEMBLED) OFFERS BENEFITS IN TRANSPORTATION AND STRENGTH, THOUGH IT IS NOT AS EASILY PORTABLE AS THE FOLDING KAYAK.

below THE INFLATABLE KAYAK IS EASY TO TRANSPORT BUT PERFORMS POORLY IN THE WIND, A CONSTANT THREAT AT SEA, AS IT IS EASILY BLOWN OFF COURSE OR EVEN BLOWN OVER. IT IS RECOMMENDED MOSTLY FOR RECREATIONAL KAYAKING IN SHELTERED AREAS.

Kayak design

A longer and narrower kayak is faster but requires more skill, whilst a short, wide craft is buoyant and stable but slower. There are many variables in kayak design that should be considered. The ideal kayak is stable but buoyant, and should be able to be smoothly maneuvered. Ultimately, it should feel comfortable and safe while it tracks a clear course through the water. In choosing a kayak, aim for a combination of elements and think of your personal priorities. If speed is not important and you plan to use your kayak in calmer conditions, these considerations should inform your choice.

Hull

The width, length and shape of the hull determines the speed, stability and tracking ability of the kayak. Some paddlers regard narrow-hulled craft as more seaworthy than wide ones because they can be leaned more easily. The wider the hull of a kayak, the more secure it feels on water, but it can be more difficult to lean, making it vulnerable to capsizing in high seas and difficult to right.

The ideal kayak offers a balance between stability and maneuverability. It should be easy for you to lean in all directions, while maintaining stability.

Keels The underside of a kayak can be rounded, flat or diamond-shaped, the shape influencing performance. The preferred shape is the shallow 'V', which offers stability and directionality. Flat is best in calm water but unstable in rough conditions, while a round bottom is maneuverable but also unstable.

Rocker The rocker of the hull refers to the shape of the keel looked at from the side. 'Rocker' describes how much higher the ends of the boat are than the middle. A kayak with more rocker is more maneuverable, and will turn faster than one with less rocker. However, kayaks with less rocker have better tracking ability. This may change when a craft with more rocker has a load which submerges more of the kayak.

Length and width

Also known as the 'beam' of a sea kayak, width makes the most noticeable difference to the feel of the craft. Beginners prefer wide kayaks for their stability but as they gain experience, their preferences may change.

In terms of length, effective single kayaks range from 4.5–5.7m (15–19ft) long, while touring doubles may be as long as 5–6.7m (17–22ft). Length impacts significantly on the kayak's performance. Generally, a shorter hull is more maneuverable but sacrifices tracking ability. Longer hulls track better and can travel

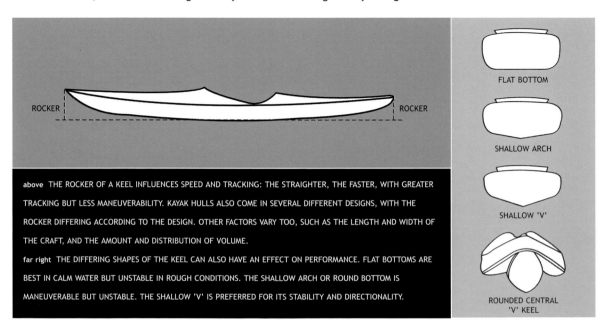

above THE ROCKER OF A KEEL INFLUENCES SPEED AND TRACKING: THE STRAIGHTER, THE FASTER, WITH GREATER TRACKING BUT LESS MANEUVERABILITY. KAYAK HULLS ALSO COME IN SEVERAL DIFFERENT DESIGNS, WITH THE ROCKER DIFFERING ACCORDING TO THE DESIGN. OTHER FACTORS VARY TOO, SUCH AS THE LENGTH AND WIDTH OF THE CRAFT, AND THE AMOUNT AND DISTRIBUTION OF VOLUME.

far right THE DIFFERING SHAPES OF THE KEEL CAN ALSO HAVE AN EFFECT ON PERFORMANCE. FLAT BOTTOMS ARE BEST IN CALM WATER BUT UNSTABLE IN ROUGH CONDITIONS. THE SHALLOW ARCH OR ROUND BOTTOM IS MANEUVERABLE BUT UNSTABLE. THE SHALLOW 'V' IS PREFERRED FOR ITS STABILITY AND DIRECTIONALITY.

ROCKER

ROCKER

FLAT BOTTOM

SHALLOW ARCH

SHALLOW 'V'

ROUNDED CENTRAL 'V' KEEL

faster than shorter ones. However, due to their greater surface friction against water, they take more effort to paddle at low speeds. Sea kayaks need to track and maneuver well, especially on rocky coasts and rough seas, and safety and comfort are dependent upon finding a workable balance between the two.

Volume and weight

You need to consider the volume of the boat in terms of your own size and how much packing space you need. The size and the distribution of a kayak's volume affect its performance. Different kayak designs concentrate the volume in different areas of the craft. Some carry most of the volume near the cockpit, allowing for narrow ends. Others carry volume far forward and back, creating fuller ends. The distribution of volume may thus influence the design of the bow.

There are two basic bow designs: a broad buoyant design that rides over waves and a narrower design that cuts through a wave.

Kayaks with volume forward and back, and a broader bow, are bouncier in small waves but more stable over large waves. They offer greater comfort than kayaks of the same maximum width but with narrower ends. Kayaks with fuller ends also carry greater loads.

Kayaks with volume in the middle and finer bows track better, cutting through waves for a smoother ride. Cutting through bigger waves, however, will create spillage of water over the deck, even submersion in big waves!

Think about the trips you plan to do and whether any one kayak will meet your needs.

Hatches and bulkheads

The closed interior spaces in the kayak are referred to as hatches. These are closed off by bulkheads and hatch covers to provide structural support, buoyancy and flotation. The front and rear bulkheads keep the kayak afloat and level after a capsize, even if the cockpit fills with water.

The disadvantage of the fold-up kayak is its lack of bulkheads: it must rely on dry bags for flotation. Sit-on kayaks are sealed units and don't necessarily

STORAGE IS LIMITED AND SAFETY ESSENTIALS CAN'T BE NEGLECTED, SO CAREFUL CONSIDERATION MUST BE GIVEN TO PACKING AND STOWING GOODS WHEN EMBARKING ON LONG TRIPS.

need bulkheads, except for separating storage compartments – and as a safety measure.

Bulkheads are made from fibreglass or foam. The former is bonded to the boat with resin, the latter is fixed with adhesive. Adhesives may detach, admitting water, while fibreglass bulkheads may create hard ridges on the hull, making it less flexible. A leaking bulkhead or one that detaches itself from the hull will threaten your safety.

Hatch covers It is advisable to have at least two hatch covers, an inner membrane and a hard outer shell. Take note of the cover and how it is secured: if straps are used, these should be strong. Rubber hatches seal neatly and require no straps. Protruding hatches act as a deflector for water pouring over the deck. Recessed hatches look neater, and the streamlining is important in rough conditions. Big hatch openings are easy to load but prone to flooding, so avoid these if you are planning long expeditions. Make sure the hatch cover is strong, and easy to shut and secure.

The foolproof and bone-dry hatch has yet to be invented, and seepage remains inevitable.

Skegs and rudders

These are not essential to kayaks but have become standard features (the rudder more so than the skeg), as they improve directionality and tracking. A skeg is simply a fin which is attached to the underside of the stern. It may be fixed or retractable and acts like the centreboard of a sailboat. It is either retracted into a slot in the rear bulkhead of the kayak or dropped into one of two positions, full or halfway, depending on conditions. Kayaks with skegs are designed for optimum maneuverability: when the skeg is up, easy turning is facilitated, but having the skeg down increases tracking in the boat.

Kayaks with foot-controlled rudders turn more easily, although not very quickly. The rudder hangs over the end of the boat or protrudes from underneath the stern. Some are designed to flip up onto the deck, allowing the paddler to travel rudderless when necessary. Flip-up rudders make landings and launches easier. They can be stored for protection during transportation, and are less likely to cause accidental injury during transportation.

Skeg or rudder?

A kayak may or may not have a skeg or rudder. If choosing between them, keep these pointers in mind:

■ Beginners, who would otherwise have to master complicated paddle strokes, find the foot-controlled rudder a boon. Even seasoned kayakers would agree that rudders are an energy-saving device on long windy passages.

■ Rudders help with both tracking and turning, while kayaks with skegs use design features such as rocker of the hull to facilitate turning.

■ Rudders have robust mechanisms, but the cables and fittings require basic maintenance, while skegs have the advantage of simplicity. Those that don't retract are prone to snagging and possible damage.

■ Skegs and rudders may interfere with maneuverability in confined spaces, making retractable ones preferable.

left A STATE-OF-THE-ART RUDDER SYSTEM SHOWS A HYDRODYNAMICALLY SHAPED BLADE RECESSED INTO THE HULL, AN ERGONOMICALLY DESIGNED YOKE AND A POSITIVE UP-AND-DOWNHAUL SYSTEM WHICH EVEN FEATURES A CONVENIENT 'CONTROL LEVER' (left below). THESE FEATURES ENABLE THE PADDLER TO MAKE FULL USE OF THE RUDDER WITHOUT UNDUE STRAIN, ENSURING A SMOOTHER AND EASIER PADDLING EXPERIENCE. ON LONG JOURNEYS A RUDDER CAN BE THE ULTIMATE ENERGY-SAVING DEVICE. WHILE MANY EXPERIENCED PADDLERS PREFER TO RELY ON THEIR OWN SKILLS FOR MANEUVERING, A RUDDER CAN BE VERY USEFUL FOR A BEGINNER. DON'T BECOME RELIANT ON IT, THOUGH, YOU SHOULD BE ABLE TO TURN WITHOUT IT.

Cockpits

While sit-on sea kayaks have seat indentations with scupper drainage holes, traditional sit-in sea kayaks have cockpits with coamings and seats mounted on the inside of the hull. Sit-in cockpits protect the lower part of the paddler's body, and offer support to the seat, thighs, knees and feet.

Cockpits may have larger or smaller openings. Small cockpits provide more support — for which you may be grateful in rough seas — but are harder to get in and out of. A neat compromise is provided by the keyhole and oval cockpits, which allow a larger opening but also have decks to brace against. Kayaks with cockpits call for special techniques for re-entering after a capsize in deep water.

The seat of a kayak is a matter of individual preference. It is vital to comfort on a long journey and, if necessary, can be replaced, although you may find that you adapt to your seat after a while.

You may customize your cockpit and seat to ensure a good fit for your hips, lower back, legs and feet. This will pay off in terms of efficiency and maneuverability.

Checklist for a good fit in a 'sit-in'

■ Have you selected the right size of kayak for your particular shape? If you are tall and well-built, you will be more comfortable in a kayak with a wider beam, while if you're slight, a narrower beam will suffice.

■ Do the cockpit and seat feel good?

■ Is the fit snug enough to allow you to maneuver the kayak?

■ Are the rudder pedals (if any) within your reach?

■ Are you able to brace your knees against the underside of the deck?

■ Are you able to paddle without strain?

■ Are you comfortable? Any slight discomfort after 15 minutes will be excruciating after 2–3 hours!

■ Has it got enough storage space to suit your needs?

■ Is your kayak sufficiently speedy, stable, and able to track well enough for the kind of sea conditions you are likely to encounter?

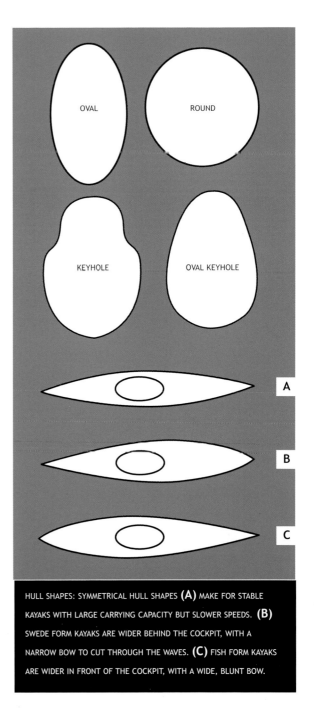

HULL SHAPES: SYMMETRICAL HULL SHAPES **(A)** MAKE FOR STABLE KAYAKS WITH LARGE CARRYING CAPACITY BUT SLOWER SPEEDS. **(B)** SWEDE FORM KAYAKS ARE WIDER BEHIND THE COCKPIT, WITH A NARROW BOW TO CUT THROUGH THE WAVES. **(C)** FISH FORM KAYAKS ARE WIDER IN FRONT OF THE COCKPIT, WITH A WIDE, BLUNT BOW.

Pay attention to the backrest; your back should be secured with the lumbar region supported and your spine held upright. Adjust the backrest before you paddle away: on a long tour your comfort is essential. If you suffer discomfort, use foam for padding those surfaces your body comes in contact with.

Pods

The pod, an innovation in kayaks with cockpits, helps to maintain flotation by reducing the amount of water entering the kayak if you capsize. It consists of a rigid, watertight capsule that attaches to the cockpit rim. The rigidity created by the pod in the centre of the boat protects the paddler if the kayak folds around a rock. A kayak without a pod may fold at the cockpit, trapping the paddler's legs, while those with pods are more likely to fold in front or behind, giving the paddler a better chance to escape. A poorly designed pod *may* trap a paddler's legs in a capsize, so keep this in mind when choosing a kayak with central consoles inside the pod.

A sock is a fabric pod that is slipped in the cockpit as a lining. The sock helps to eliminate flooding, and keeps the paddler warm, but it may be cumbersome and may make it difficult to enter the cockpit.

Kayaks for touring

When buying a kayak for long trips, don't get overwhelmed by technical details. Research shows that the differences in performance — whether speed, tracking, efficiency or stability — among touring kayaks are slight at the pace of most paddlers. So, how the boat feels, whether it is stable and has enough storage space, and how neatly you fit into it are the most important features. Only if you are busy planning long coastal trips which require you to reduce your exposure to the sea and the varying climatic conditions, should the question of speed over comfort and versatility be considered.

For long trips you need to give some serious thought to food, water and camping equipment. If you are travelling to cold places, you must take warm clothing and more protective bedding. If your planned route is along a desert coastline, you'll need more water and sun protection than usual. These trips demand significant packing space, in contrast with short tours in moderate climates, which call for less storage.

In thinking about the volume of the hull, consider its strength and weight too. While boats are becoming lighter and weight does not necessarily equal strength, one needs to know that a lightweight model is strong enough to withstand harsh conditions. While lightness has its advantages, weight is also important in the sea. Moving fast over large waves leaves portions of the kayak suspended in the air, which is more difficult to

TRAVELLING IN LARGE GROUPS, AND IN DOUBLE KAYAKS, INCREASES SAFETY, AND CAN CREATE A FUN TOURING EXPERIENCE. TOURING KAYAKS MUST BE STRONG, ROBUST AND SUITABLE FOR THE CONDITIONS THEY WILL BE USED IN — THE PROPER EQUIPMENT IS VITAL.

control in a light kayak. The deck of a sea kayak should be strong enough to bear the weight of a distressed fellow kayaker in a rescue.

Additional fittings

Innovative features that contribute to safety, comfort and ease in transporting and paddling a kayak are now widely available. These include:

■ Toggles for carrying kayaks are made of plastic or wood, and are attached to the top and bottom ends of the craft. Toggles should be well secured and make a boat easier to carry or tow. In some countries, regulations require a kayak to have strong attachment points for towing before it is considered seaworthy.

■ Perimeter or deck-lines are becoming increasingly popular. They're designed to be held onto during launches, landings and rescues, and are useful for securing loose items. Perimeter lines are made of nonelastic rope and should ideally fit into a shallow recess around the perimeter of the deck.

■ Paddle-parks consist of rigging systems on the rear deck to which paddles may be secured during a paddle-float rescue.

Looking after your boat

Check all the components of your boat regularly. Plastic boats should be examined for hairline cracks which indicate that the plastic is becoming brittle. Check rudder fittings, deck lines, hatch covers and buoyancy bags and replace when necessary to avoid dealing with breakages at sea. Follow these key rules to increase the longevity of your kayak:

■ Rinse the kayak thoroughly with fresh water.
■ Use a mild soap to clean the outside; never scrub boats with abrasives.
■ Fibreglass or kevlar hulls should be waxed once or twice a year to shine and protect them.
■ Gelcoats may be restored every few years by buffing with a fine-grade rubbing compound.
■ Do not hesitate to repair dents, using one of the handy repair guides available.

KAYAKS MAY BE STORED OUT OF THE WAY AS SIMPLY AS SHOWN ABOVE, ALTHOUGH POLYTHENE KAYAKS WILL WARP IF LEFT IN THIS POSITION FOR LONGER THAN A DAY AND SHOULD PREFERABLY BE HUNG UPSIDE DOWN. ELABORATE PULLEY SYSTEMS OR COMMERCIALLY AVAILABLE RACK SYSTEMS MAY BE USED FOR EASY STORAGE AND RETRIEVAL.

Storage

These minimum precautions will ensure that you have maximum paddling time and enjoyment when you take to the water in your kayak. Bear in mind that fibreglass kayaks are easy to store — they maintain their shape and are resistant to damage.

■ Store the kayak out of sunlight as it damages the materials. If necessary, rig up an awning for shade.
■ Don't use plastic covers, which create a 'greenhouse effect' that will accelerate deterioration.
■ Store the kayak keel up, which makes it easier to clean. Prop it on blocks or hang it up in a sling.
■ In a dry environment, storing the craft with the cockpit cover and hatches on will keep out dust. If the kayak is damp, allow air to circulate.
■ Folding kayaks should be stored unfolded. Keep the hull in a cool, well-ventilated place and dust with talcum powder to absorb damp.
■ Inflatable kayaks should ideally be stored inflated.

Equipping Yourself

it takes more than a kayak to prepare you for your first excursion. There is a wide array of equipment to choose from and the right gear will add greatly to your fun and safety on the water.

Paddles

Your choice of paddle will have an influence on your performance, comfort, safety and mobility. To be effective, a paddle must have certain characteristics:

- It should be comfortable to hold and manipulate
- It should be strong enough to bear your weight in a paddle-float rescue
- A strong, well-shaped shaft will protect your hands and improve your grip
- The blade should enter the water smoothly, without creating excessive splash
- A good quality sea kayak paddle should weigh between 1kg (40oz) and 0.8kg (30oz). Less will compromise its strength, more will create excess weight.

When choosing a paddle, consider the kayak it will be used with (wider kayaks need longer paddles, narrower ones, shorter paddles); the conditions in which it will be used; and the height, strength and arm-length of the paddler. You don't need to choose the top-of-the-range paddle for recreational cruising, but do select a reliable paddle.

In the case of a double kayak, it is important to balance the needs of both paddlers. The correct paddles can compensate for an imbalance in the partners' strengths. You may find that a short, narrow-bladed paddle (smaller surface area) for the weaker paddler and a long, large-bladed one for the stronger paddler achieve such balance.

Materials for Paddles

Paddles are made from a variety of materials. Wood paddles are attractive and strong. They are generally heavier than synthetic paddles, but some come in at under 1.5kg (50oz). They are prone to water retention, and thus need regular varnishing. Among a wide range of synthetic paddles are those made of fibreglass or carbon fibre. While not as attractive as wooden paddles, they are generally well-designed for strength, lightness and durability. The all-carbon type is light in weight but not on the pocket! For an economical compromise, there is the fibreglass-shafted paddle with carbon blades, which also reduces overall weight. However these must be custom-made.

Polyfibre blades, which are extruded and pop-riveted to the shaft, are durable and affordable. Polycarbon versions, which are strong but lightweight, are also available.

above PADDLE SHAFTS MAY BE ALUMINIUM, FIBREGLASS OR WOOD, WITH BLADES OF CARBON-FIBRE **(A)**, FIBREGLASS **(B)**, PLASTIC **(C)**, OR POLYCARBON. **top** A KAYAK HARNESSING AN INNOVATIVE DHOW RIG. **right** USING A SPINNAKER-TYPE RIG FOR SAILING.

PADDLES MAY BE FEATHERED OR unfeathered. Feathered blades are set at an angle of up to 90 degrees to each other. Unfeathered paddles have blades on one plane.

Advantages and disadvantages

■ When travelling into the wind, feathering reduces windage on the paddle blades

■ Feathered paddles are adapted for racing kayaks, being strong when used with short paddles and narrow kayaks

■ Feathered paddles are harder on the wrists than unfeathered ones. On long trips, feathered paddles can increase the risk of tenosynovitis (inflammation of the tendons of the wrist)

■ If the wind is behind the paddler, unfeathered blades make use of it to provide a boost

■ When the wind comes from the side, unfeathered blades are less affected than feathered

Shape

The shape of the blade affects its overall performance. Broad, large-bladed paddles, especially if asymmetric or of the 'wing'

top A LONG, NARROW BLADE REDUCES STRAIN ON THE ARMS.

centre AN ASYMMETRICAL BLADE — FOR MAXIMUM POWER.

bottom A SYMMETRICAL BLADE FOR HASSLE-FREE MANOEUVRING.

variety, are powerful when used with light, fast kayaks, particularly when there is little wind. A wide blade offers more power per

stroke and more surface area for bracing and rolling. It is the paddle of choice for racing conditions, but is not usually recommended for sea kayaking.

With heavily laden kayaks these blades are less effective and put additional strain on the paddler. The narrow paddle is less vulnerable to wind and copes well with heavy loads. It is less stressful to use for extended periods and reduces the chance of injury to wrists or elbows. This makes it ideal for long-distance travel in areas where exposure to the elements is inevitable. It is important to stick with a paddle that works well for you as sudden changes may cause injury or confusion.

Length

The length of the paddle is another important factor. The factors that determine choice here are the body size and strength of

Basic paddle parts

Paddle length and weight, and blade shape are all considerations in choosing the right paddle for your needs. Paddles are available in a wide range of shapes and sizes, so take the time to choose one for your paddling style.

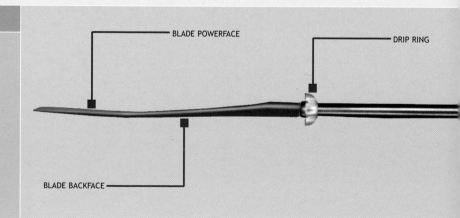

BLADE POWERFACE

DRIP RING

BLADE BACKFACE

the paddler and the size of the kayak. Paddle lengths vary from 210–260cm (83–102in), averaging about 216–224cm (85–88in). Longer paddles provide more power but create problems for smaller paddlers or when used with narrow kayaks. Double kayaks, with their wider beams, need longer paddles to avoid banging the hull when paddling. Longer paddles tend to increase the side-to-side rolling of the kayak.

Since you may spend many hours gripping your paddle, its weight and balance are essential to your comfort. Light paddles will be less of a strain but are more fragile. A paddle grip may also enhance your comfort, but could interfere with the versatility of a symmetrical paddle.

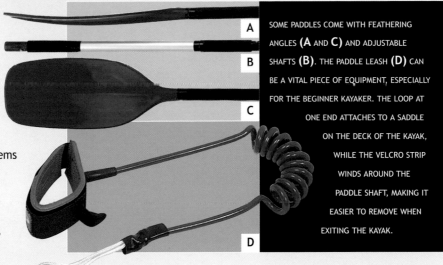

A

B

C

D

SOME PADDLES COME WITH FEATHERING ANGLES (**A** AND **C**) AND ADJUSTABLE SHAFTS (**B**). THE PADDLE LEASH (**D**) CAN BE A VITAL PIECE OF EQUIPMENT, ESPECIALLY FOR THE BEGINNER KAYAKER. THE LOOP AT ONE END ATTACHES TO A SADDLE ON THE DECK OF THE KAYAK, WHILE THE VELCRO STRIP WINDS AROUND THE PADDLE SHAFT, MAKING IT EASIER TO REMOVE WHEN EXITING THE KAYAK.

Paddle leashes

A leash tethers the paddle to the kayak or to the paddler's wrist. Leashes may have Velcro collars or may be a simple loop design. They are usually fixed to the forward deck rigging with a snap shackle. Leashes allow you to free your hands by releasing the paddle without losing it — giving you the opportunity to take a break when your arms need relieving. The paddle is also retrievable if dropped or blown out of your hands. If you lose your grip on the kayak after a wet exit, and the wind or the waves take it, a paddle dragging in the water may help to slow it down. However, a leash may be an encumbrance to your paddling style, and could take some getting used to.

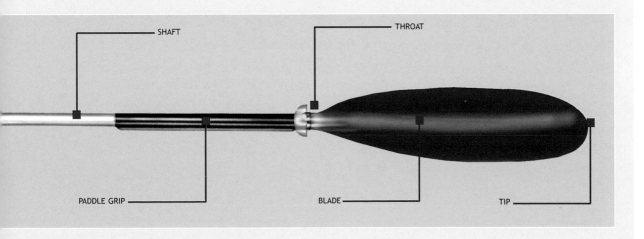

SHAFT

THROAT

PADDLE GRIP

BLADE

TIP

Personal Flotation Devices (PFDs)

PFDs are essential for kayakers and need to conform to various national codes. They are a legal requirement in almost all countries, and some qualities, like colour, materials and features, may be prescribed. When purchasing a PFD, ask for an approved model. The two main varieties are:

Regular padded flotation jacket This offers protection against cold water and bad weather. It is economical, readily available in comfortable, utilitarian designs with extras like pockets and attachment points. It cannot be punctured and is the jacket of choice for most paddlers.

Inflatable buoyancy jacket This is comfortable to paddle in when deflated and its carbon dioxide cartridge makes it instantly inflatable by tugging a ring. It may also be inflated by mouth, and it is preferable to have both options, so check this when buying one.

These jackets can be worn over a wet or a dry suit to prevent hypothermia. They may be inflated for resting or deflated for swimming. However, it is possible that the cartridge may fail to inflate. Inflatable jackets are also vulnerable to puncture, so must be carefully stored and used. These are not the safest jackets to use in rough sea conditions.

Look after your jacket well — your life may depend on it. Do not compress the flotation material when packing it and ensure it is well rinsed and dried before storage to preserve the material, avoid rusting and protect the stitching.

Sprayskirts and spraydecks

Sprayskirts are designed to prevent water from entering the cockpit. The skirt fits snugly from the paddler's chest to the cockpit's coaming (rim), and adjustable shoulder straps or a firm neoprene waistband prevent it from falling down. The skirt needs to be attached firmly enough to withstand waves breaking over the kayak but should be easily removed with a tug when necessary. It should be fitted with release loops for ease of removal in the event of a capsize. The skirt may be fitted with a zipper that slides from chest to

Some tips for choosing a PFD

■ The fit is important — ideally snug but not tight.

■ It shouldn't chafe particularly at the armholes.

■ It shouldn't ride up to your chin when you're seated.

■ It shouldn't be too long to fit over the sprayskirt.

■ It must not slip over your head when you are in the water — some have crotch straps to prevent this.

■ It should have at least one pocket, preferably more, for keeping some safety items handy (flares, a knife), although in some countries pockets are prohibited.

■ PFDs are not the same as life jackets, which are prescribed for commercial shipping and have to meet strict regulations in terms of design and flotation.

above A PFD SUITABLE FOR SEA KAYAKING FEATURES A SIDE ZIP FOR SLIPPING ON EASILY, ADJUSTABLE NEOPRENE SHOULDER AND WAIST BANDS FOR COMFORT AND WARMTH, EXPANDED POCKETS WITH DRAINAGE ON CHEST AND BACK, CROTCH STRAPS, AND AN APPROVED COLOUR, MATERIAL AND STITCHING. ATTACHMENT POINTS FOR A WHISTLE, KNIFE AND ADDITIONAL FLARES MAKE THIS PURPOSE-DESIGNED BUOYANCY AND UTILITY JACKET A GREAT IMPROVEMENT ON THE OLD KAYAKING LIFE-JACKET LYING IN MANY AN ATTIC.

deck, so that you can reach for something or enter and leave the kayak without detaching the skirt from the cockpit rim. A variation of the sprayskirt is an anorak which attaches to the cockpit.

Sprayskirts are usually made of coated nylon or neoprene. Nylon is light and comfortable but can sag, collecting water. Neoprene is more waterproof, heavier and warmer. It is better for cold conditions but more rigid, and difficult to get on and off. A separate nylon cockpit cover is useful to keep the cockpit clean and dry during transportation and storage, and converts the cockpit into a storage bin for the PFD and sprayskirt.

Spraydecks Some folding kayaks are equipped with these watertight cockpit covers, which protect larger areas than sprayskirts and need to be securely attached to the kayak.

Storage bags and boxes

No matter how watertight your bulkheads or hatches are, water can seep in. A wide range of containers has been designed for sea kayaks. Bags are useful: they organize your gear when travelling and keep things dry,

essential to comfort, even to survival, in cold climates. They also provide buoyancy in the event of leakages or capsizes. Some are designed to be inflated after loading and inflation tubes should be accessible for topping up with air while travelling. For maximum buoyancy, the bags should fill as much space as possible. Most bags are made of PVC.

Some pointers for storage bags are as follows:

- Must be waterproof and sturdy, to resist snagging
- Must seal tightly. The best bags close with a top that rolls down and fastens with buckles
- Should fit snugly into storage spaces — some are tapered to fit kayaks
- Should be attached to the kayak, especially if mounted on the deck, so they don't float away if it capsizes

Tough plastic storage boxes are also available. Small ones are easy to access and organize; first-aid and tool kits work well in the smaller boxes. Some have latex collars for a watertight seal.

DRY BAGS COME IN VARIOUS SIZES AND MATERIALS WITH DIFFERENT SEALING SYSTEMS. A TRANSPARENT BAG (RIGHT) OFFERS A USEFUL ADDED FEATURE. DRY BAGS ARE ESSENTIAL FOR KEEPING YOUR GEAR DRY AND ORGANIZED.

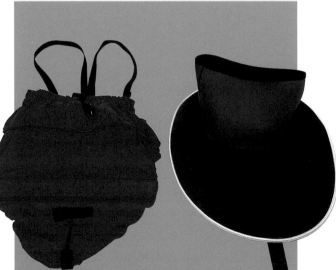

above left A LIGHTWEIGHT NYLON SPRAYSKIRT WITH SHOULDER BRACES, SUITABLE FOR MILD CONDITIONS.
above right A FIRM AND STURDY HIGH-QUALITY NEOPRENE SPRAYSKIRT FOR MORE INCLEMENT WEATHER AND SEA CONDITIONS.

Clothing

SAFETY AND PRACTICALITY govern the kayaker's dress code — the paddler dresses for comfort and to keep as dry as possible. Bear in mind both air and sea temperature — there's every chance of a dunking. Clothing also screens paddlers from the sun.

You don't want to feel restricted by clothing. Loose, quick-drying wind- and waterproof garments are ideal. Paddling will warm you up fast, so wear layers which you can peel off. Keep warmer clothes to hand in case the temperature drops. If you stop for a while, you'll cool off rapidly.

Wet or dry suits

There's no question about it, paddlers get wet! So you may want to wear a wet or a dry suit. Farmer Johns, tight-fitting all-in-one neoprene trousers and a high-neck top, are popular in colder climates. In warmer areas wet-suit shorts worn with a windbreaker are ideal. The wet-suit allows in a thin layer of water, which is quickly warmed by your body and insulates you from the cold water outside. Nevertheless, wet-suits have certain disadvantages:

■ A Farmer John has limited capacity to keep you warm in cold seas
■ It stays damp and smelly on long trips
■ It needs to be worn constantly

■ The wet suit limits your freedom to urinate

Dry suits are loose-fitting, made of vinyl and may consist of one or two pieces. They have waterproof latex seals at all openings and waterproof zippers across the chest or back. Dry suits are comfortable, they stay dry in rain and markedly increase survival time in cold seas. The effectiveness of the dry suit depends on what is worn underneath it, so for maximum insulation against icy water, one needs more layers of clothing than is comfortable for paddling.

When making a choice of fabrics: wool or synthetics are good in the wet; cotton is a good choice in warm weather, but in the cold it is slow to dry, retains damp and offers little thermal protection when wet.

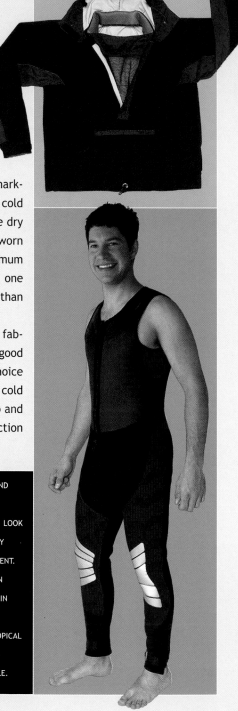

top PADDLING JACKETS ARE USEFUL AND ARE AVAILABLE IN DEGREES OF WATER-TIGHTNESS TO SUIT VARIOUS CLIMATES. LOOK FOR GOOD QUALITY GARMENTS AS THEY SHOULD BE HARD-WORKING AND RESILIENT.
right THE FARMER JOHN IS POPULAR IN COLDER CLIMATES, BUT FOR PADDLING IN ARCTIC CONDITIONS, THE DRY SUIT IS RECOMMENDED. IN WARMER, MORE TROPICAL AREAS, WET-SUIT SHORTS AND A WIND-BREAKER WOULD BE THE MOST SUITABLE.

Paddling jackets

These are often combined with a Farmer John wet suit. They are waterproof nylon windcheaters with neck and wrist cuffs that seal against water. They are frequently fitted with 'kangaroo pouches' for storing things, while some have detachable hoods.

Head gear

It is important to keep your head warm — most body heat is lost via the head and neck. A wool or fleece hat is essential when it's chilly. On very cold days a neoprene cap is useful if you fall in; a cheap alternative is a woolly hat worn over a swimcap. In strong sun, wear a hat with a brim wide enough to shade your face and neck. Sunglasses should be functional rather than fashionable. Even in icy conditions, glare strains your eyes. A cap with an extended front visor, a neck flap and lanyard for securing it will make paddling in direct sunshine more comfortable. Always wear a helmet when practising surfing skills, and in rocky areas with surf.

Hand and foot gear

Keep your hands warm and protected. In wet or icy conditions, leather gloves are comfortable and grip well. Neoprene gloves, with articulated fingers and grips on the palms, are also effective. 'Pogies' are neoprene/nylon mittens, designed to cover the top of the hand; they are fitted over the paddle shaft. They protect hands while permitting a barehand grip on the paddle. In a capsize your hands may come out of them. Lycra sailing or cycling gloves will prevent blisters and sunburn and offer an affordable option. For wrist protection, wear spats — neoprene tubes that seal the cuffs of your anorak — although these may cause rashes if worn for long trips. Feet must be protected from abrasive surfaces and cold. Wear rubber boots or wet suit bootees with hard soles. Bear in mind that hiking sandals with straps can interfere with pedal control.

Sun protection gear

In strong sunshine the whole body must be adequately protected. Sunscreen is essential. Wear the highest protection factors, even if it's overcast. Don't neglect extremities such as your hands and feet, especially if you're on a sit-on kayak. Adequate headgear will also protect your head and neck from sunburn.

It is worth your while to invest in quality lightweight, durable clothing to wear on kayak tours.

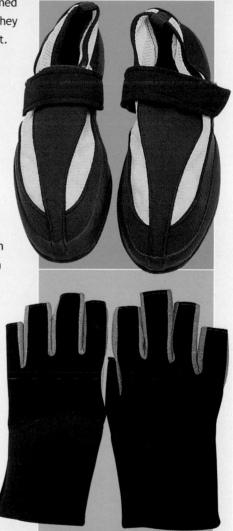

top BOOTEES MUST BE COMFORTABLE AND SHOULD PROVIDE PROTECTION FOR THE SOLES AND UPPER FOOT, BUT MUST ALLOW FOR ENOUGH SENSITIVITY TO CONTROL THE RUDDER SYSTEM'S PEDALS. **bottom** MITTENS AND 'POGIES' (NEOPRENE) STAVE OFF BLISTERS, COLD AND SUNBURN. THE IDEAL GLOVES ARE NEOPRENE OR LEATHER AND LYCRA.

above WITH A COMPASS YOU CAN CHECK YOUR COURSE.

above right THIS LIGHTWEIGHT ANEMOMETER JUDGES WIND SPEED —
AND WHETHER CONDITIONS ARE WITHIN YOUR CAPABILITY.

right A MECHANICAL BAROMETER READS ATMOSPHERIC PRESSURE SO YOU
CAN PREDICT WEATHER CHANGES.

Kayaking essentials

One paddler's necessity may be another's indulgence but, generally, most paddlers would find the following items useful to take along:

Compass

This is essential for navigation. A compass enables you to track your route by aiming your kayak towards the point you're making for, taking a reading, and sticking with it. It is recommended that the compass be mounted on the kayak's deck (some kayaks have specially moulded compass mounts). For chart navigation you'll need an orienteering compass as well, while a lighted compass is great for moonless nights. Remember, your compass may give false readings if it is near a metal object.

Barometer and anemometer

You can be your own weatherman with these two instruments. A barometer reads atmospheric pressure, a reliable means of predicting changes in weather. Digital barometers have the advantage of demonstrating trends over 24 hours by means of bar graphs.

Anemometers measure wind speed, which may indicate whether it is safe to go out in a kayak. It is generally accepted that recreational craft such as sea kayaks are suitable for conditions up to Force 4 on the Beaufort Wind Scale (0–16 knots or 30kph).

Binoculars

Binoculars are essential to safety and as an aid to navigation and identification. They are also great for whale- or bird-watching. Keep waterproof binoculars handy, attached to the deck or your PFD with a lanyard. Compact ones are ideal.

Sealed, nitrogen-purged binoculars are protected against interior condensation.

Repair kit

It is advisable to carry the appropriate materials and repairing tools when you embark on a journey. Two tips: duct tape can be used for temporary repairs, and a few metres of cord can stand in for broken rudder cables. It is worth your while to obtain a good book on kayak repair, and to always make sure you have all the necessary tools for repairing your own kayak.

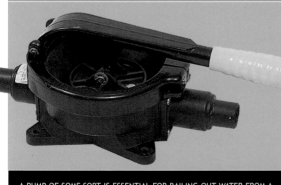

A PUMP OF SOME SORT IS ESSENTIAL FOR BAILING OUT WATER FROM A KAYAK AND THERE ARE VARIOUS MODELS AVAILABLE. A REMOTE PUMP (TOP AND CENTRE) IS MOBILE AND CAN BE USED WHEREVER WATER COLLECTS. THIS MODEL CAN EXPEL 25 LITRES (52PT) IN ONE MINUTE UNDER IDEAL CONDITIONS. A DECK-MOUNTED PUMP (ABOVE) IS ALSO EFFICIENT, AND IF MOUNTED TOPSIDE CAN BE OPERATED WITHOUT HAVING TO RELEASE THE SPRAYSKIRT.

Bilge pump

Kayakers must be resigned to having some water in their kayak, but too much may prove dangerous. Every paddler on the sea needs a means of bailing out water. In many countries, this is a legal requirement for sea-worthiness. There are various methods:

Most common is using a container to scoop water out of the kayak. This is not easily achieved while you're in the kayak as the sprayskirt must be parted from the cockpit rim. In bad weather, more water may come in than can be bailed.

A **cylindrical remote bilge pump** is efficient and can be used with the sprayskirt in place. The pump, when braced against the thigh, can be operated with one hand. It is particularly useful for getting water out of hard-to-reach areas. Built-in pumps, fixed to the kayak so they can't fall overboard, use a lever for pumping water. They are very effective, provided the water is over the inlet pipe.

Foot-operated pumps can be installed on the foot brace, allowing one to clear the water whilst paddling.

Electric pumps provide effortless pumping and are efficient, if the battery doesn't run out when you need it most. Always carry a manual pump too! Each cockpit of a double kayak needs a pump.

Flotation devices

Paddle float Essential safety equipment should include this float, which fits over one blade of the paddle and can be used as an outrigger to stabilize the kayak. In the event of a wet exit (falling out of a kayak into the water), the float is fitted over one blade while the opposite end of the paddle rests on the rear deck, behind the cockpit. This arrangement supports you as you climb back in. Some kayaks have a 'paddle-park' to facilitate this maneuver. Paddle float rescue techniques are discussed in Getting on the Water.

Sea Wings These tube-shaped floats are inflated and fixed on each side of the cockpit to increase the kayak's stability. If a paddler is injured, Sea Wings can keep the kayak steady until help arrives.

BackUP This is a bag with a supply of carbon dioxide, which can be stored on the front deck. In the event of a capsize, yanking a ring-pull will inflate the bag in seconds. Leaning on the bag helps to right the kayak. The BackUP needs a fresh cartridge for each use.

Taking care of your gear

Your gear keeps you safe and comfortable at sea, so take care of it.

■ Rinse all gear with fresh water to remove salt and sand.
■ Neoprene shampoo is useful for cleaning sprayskirts and wet suits.
■ Check your gear for wear and tear; fix ruptures or breakages immediately.
■ Monitor items that date, like batteries, and replace in good time.
■ Everything must be bone-dry before storing.

Store all gear in a clean, dry place where air circulates freely. For maximum protection, keep your paddles in one of the attractive protective cases available. These will look good, protect paddles from dirt and sun, and make transportation easier. Store other items in cupboards, boxes or bins. Powders or dessicants keep stored gear dry. Your equipment should be organized, clean and easily retrievable.

Tow lines

A tow line is a system of line and links for towing other craft. The most effective ones are ready-made but a length of strong line can also be used. Lines should be 6–10m (20–35ft) long for safe towing, although a shorter line offers less resistance. Tow lines used to stretch from the stern of the kayak to the bow toggle of the kayak being towed. Nowadays, they usually link to your waist-belt, allowing for quick release. A tow line is designed for situations such as towing a kayak when the paddler has been injured, keeping a capsized kayak and paddler away from a rough lee shore, or stabilizing a capsized kayak while the paddler re-enters and bails water out.

A MODERN REAR MOUNTED TOWING SYTEM WITH A QUICK RELEASE JAM CLEAT AND CENTRE TOWING EYE IS A USEFUL EXTRA ITEM OF SAFETY EQUIPMENT.

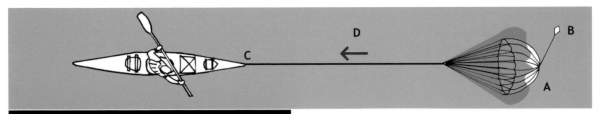

Sea anchors

There is great debate over the size, design and suitability of sea anchors for small craft at sea. Some paddlers regard the sea anchor as essential, and underrated, equipment for sea kayaking. In reality, however, they are seldom deployed by recreational kayakers. Nevertheless, they may prove useful.

The sea anchor, or drogue, looks like a small parachute that fills with water when deployed from the kayak's bow. This creates resistance to slow the downwind drift of the kayak, while keeping the kayak facing into the wind to lessen the impact of waves. Sea anchors made specially for kayaks are stored on the front deck. They come in handy for:

■ Assisting in a paddle float rescue in rough seas
■ Taking a break during an upwind stretch without finding yourself back where you started!
■ Keeping the kayak static while fishing or bird-watching
■ Turning the craft upwind in a gale

Knives

A top-quality, sharp knife which can be opened with one hand will be invaluable in a wide range of situations. Keep the knife secure yet accessible, preferably attached to the deck or your PFD with a lanyard.

Avoid the temptation to damage the blade by opening oysters with it because when you need a knife most, it needs to be a sharp one! A multiple-tool-type knife can prove invaluable.

Medical kit

Buy or assemble a first-aid kit, particularly if you plan to take long tours. The kit should include all the basic instruments and medical supplies in case of an accident or emergency situation (including vacuum-packed syringes and drip kits for longer journeys). You will also need high-factor sunscreen, seasickness pills and appropriate medication (malaria tablets where relevant) and equipment for the area you will be travelling in.

Medical recommended basics

■ bandages and adhesive bandage strips or surgical tape in assorted sizes, including butterfly bandages
■ elastic wraps
■ adhesive tape
■ sterile cotton balls, eye patches and gauze pads
■ absorbent cotton
■ triangular bandage for wrapping injuries and making an arm sling
■ scissors with rounded or blunt-tipped edges
■ tweezers
■ cotton-tipped swabs
■ space blanket
■ thermometer
■ paracetamol tablets
■ antiseptic solution, such as hydrogen peroxide, or wipes, to clean a superficial wound
■ antibiotic ointment or spray
■ calamine lotion or hydrocortisone cream
■ eye drops
■ first-aid manual
■ flashlight
■ tissues, soap, safety pins
■ disposable latex gloves

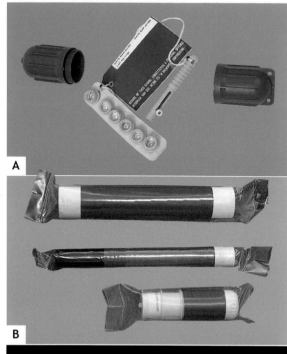

EASILY CARRIED PENCIL FLARES **(A)** CAN FIT INTO A PFD POCKET. YOU SHOULD ALSO CARRY HAND-HELD OR PARACHUTE FLARES **(B)** AS PENCIL FLARES ALONE MAY NOT BE ENOUGH. FLARES ARE ESSENTIAL SAFETY EQUIPMENT FOR PADDLERS AND YOU SHOULD ALWAYS CARRY AN ASSORTMENT, EASILY ACCESSIBLE IN CASE OF EMERGENCY.

Flares and signalling devices

Listed below are the main types of flares. Other signalling devices can be used to complement these, and most of them are compact enough to be strapped to your person or kayak. Try to carry a few kinds of devices for differing situations. It is useful to have a range of flares available.

Meteor flares release bright flares which shoot up 100–150m (330–490ft) into the sky. They alert rescuers and indicate your whereabouts, offering many advantages.

- They are compact
- They are waterproof, cheap and easily available
- They are highly visible at night, and also effective in daylight

Parachute flare are powerful flares launched from a hand-held tube. At about 300m (1000ft) up, the flare ignites and opens its parachute, shining brightly for 30 seconds as it floats down. It is effective, but expensive and bulky.

Hand-held flares shine longer than aerial flares but are not as visible from a distance. They are useful for guiding rescuers to your exact location.

Smoke flares emit brightly coloured smoke, which assists in attracting help while indicating wind direction.

Signal mirror. Simple and reliable, the signal mirror will continue to signal your location for as long as you need it to, provided that sunlight is available. Once it is clear that rescuers have seen you, stop flashing — to avoid blinding your rescuers. There are sophisticated signal mirrors that have siting-holes or 'red dots' for accuracy.

Strobes are battery-operated torches, which are useful in darkness, and can flash for hours, pinpointing your location for as long as the batteries last. Waterproof strobes are relatively cheap, but more sophisticated versions are more reliable and offer visibility over greater distances.

Dye markers release a powder that stains the water around your kayak a fluorescent green. This assists airborne rescuers in locating you. But beware, in rough seas the dye disperses fast!

Distress flags are PVC flags that direct your rescuer to your exact location and are less ephemeral than dye. They are usually packaged in plastic tubes, are large and float easily.

Whistles and horns. Air horns, though bulky, are louder than whistles and are essential for attracting attention or warning approaching craft if you get caught in fog. You can also communicate with fellow kayakers.

Communication

Radios serve the kayaker well when communication with fellow paddlers, or the wider world, is called for. Very high frequency (VHF) radios are specifically designed for short-range two-way communication. They work in a limited radius of 10–20km (6–12 miles) within line-of-sight. VHF radios use rechargeable battery packs, which are fairly long-lived. For extended trips, pack a charged spare. VHF radios require Radio Operators' Certificates, call signs and licenses. Radio procedures are rigorous and must be followed — Channel 16 (VHF) and Channel A (UHF) are call and emergency channels.

Even within their limitations, VHF radios are handy in certain situations, for:

- communicating with paddling partners
- communication in areas of heavy sea-traffic
- monitoring weather reports
- helping rescuers locate you in emergencies
- informing rescuers of your condition

Ultra High Frequency (UHF-FM) radios, on the other hand, are intended for communication within a group, not for summoning aid.

The Emergency Position Indicating Radio Beacon (EPIRB) emits signals which, when received by rescuers, direct them to your position. The EPIRB is a one-way radio transmitter that sends a signal to an orbiting network of satellites checked by ground monitoring stations involved in rescue missions. EPIRBs can elicit assistance from much greater distances than radios, making them vital for anyone touring isolated areas, but they are generally still too expensive for recreational paddlers.

A disadvantage is that, although the signals have long range, you can only be sure your signal has been picked up when help arrives.

Cellphones have become essential items for kayakers, particularly in emergency situations. A vast network of satellites is available to cellphone users, even offshore or in remote areas. Get to know the emergency telephone numbers of the country you are in.

As yet, there are no waterproof phones, so make sure your cellphone is kept in a waterproof container. Programme in all emergency numbers and keep your PIN (Personal Identity Number) in the waterproof bag so your rescuer can use the phone in the event that you are incapacitated.

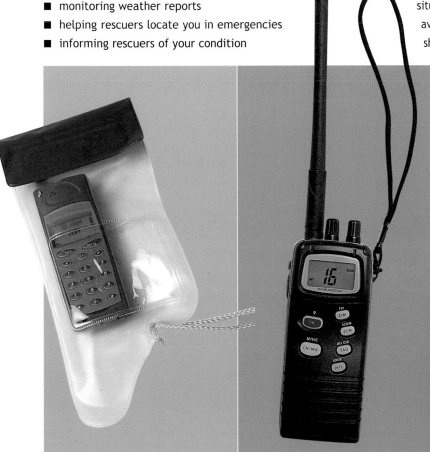

far left WATERPROOF POUCHES ARE AVAILABLE TO PROTECT YOUR RADIO OR CELLPHONE. THE POUCHES COME IN VARIOUS DESIGNS, AND THE DEVICE NEED NOT BE REMOVED FOR COMMUNICATION. THESE MUST BE WELL-SEALED AND KEPT OUT OF DIRECT SUNLIGHT TO AVOID CONDENSATION OCCURRING INSIDE THEM. **left** A WATER-RESISTANT VHF RADIO FOR TWO-WAY COMMUNICATION ENHANCES SAFETY.

Getting on the Water

having mastered paddling on calmer waters, you're ready for the challenge of the ocean waves. However, even if paddling a kayak comes naturally to you, it is essential that you master some basic techniques and practical skills before you safely embark on a trip on the ocean. To begin with, you need to get the kayak to the water.

Transporting a kayak by road

If you are using your regular vehicle, you will require a roof rack for one or two kayaks, or a trailer for several kayaks. There are many options for roof racks and trailers available, so shop around to find the system that best suits your needs and your pocket.

If you install a roof rack, space the crossbars as far apart as possible to spread support for the kayak. When loading your kayak on the roof racks, there are a number of things to bear in mind:

■ If you are loading more than one kayak, make sure that they are parallel to each other, facing the same direction as the car
■ Position the kayaks at the centre of the roof rack and avoid chafing of the hulls by keeping them apart
■ Kayaks should be firmly (not tightly) secured; tight straps may cause damage
■ Straps are preferable to ropes — they chafe less and secure a wider area of the kayak. Self-locking buckles offer a secure grip
■ Tie the ends of the kayak to prevent it from lifting or being blown sideways
■ Use the cockpit cover and secure the hatch covers to protect kayaks from rain and dust
■ Set the rudder so that it doesn't catch the wind, which may bend the blade
■ Secure the kayak against theft with a chain or cable lock; some roof racks have integral locks

■ Don't travel with a laden kayak; it will be heavy, and gear may be blown away or stolen
■ Keep an eye on the kayak while travelling and check it when you stop

Lifting the kayak onto the roof rack is easy when you know how. It may be loaded from the side or from the back. To load a kayak from the side: place the kayak next to the car, and about 1m (3ft) away — the bow should extend about 1.5m (5ft) beyond the forward rack. Holding the kayak sideways, lift the bow onto the rack at the front. Now lift the stern onto the rear rack and slide it into position. (Some rack systems have hinged arms which swivel out to provide support while loading. Racks may also be custom-made with rollers for easy loading.)

To load a kayak from the back: put the kayak on the ground behind the car with the stern in line with, and the bow slightly off to one side of, the vehicle. (A towel under the stern on the car body will prevent scratches.) First lift the bow and slide it onto the rear roof rack, now lift the stern and push the kayak forwards into place, shifting it along gently if it doesn't slide easily. Take extra care if the wind is blowing from the side, and tie the craft down quickly, preferably with assistance from a partner.

above IT IS ESSENTIAL TO ENSURE THAT YOUR KAYAKS ARE SECURELY MOUNTED ON THE ROOF RACKS OF YOUR VEHICLE. KAYAKS MAY BE TIED WITH ROPE OR WITH STRAPS, RESTING ON EITHER THE HULL OR THE DECK. CRADLES AS SHOWN HERE KEEP THE KAYAK SECURE AND PREVENT DENTING AND CHAFING.
right A MODERN SIT-ON KAYAK WITH HATCHES FORE AND AFT FOR STORAGE AND A FLIP-UP RUDDER STANDS READY ON THE BEACH IN MOSSEL BAY, SOUTH AFRICA. IN GENTLE CONDITIONS SUCH AS THOSE PICTURED HERE, IT IS EASY TO LAUNCH A KAYAK OUT THROUGH SURF.

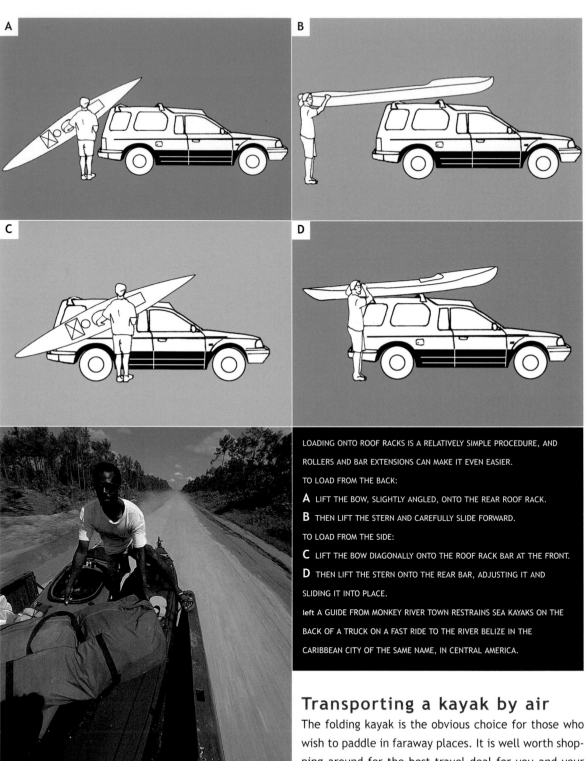

LOADING ONTO ROOF RACKS IS A RELATIVELY SIMPLE PROCEDURE, AND ROLLERS AND BAR EXTENSIONS CAN MAKE IT EVEN EASIER.

TO LOAD FROM THE BACK:

A LIFT THE BOW, SLIGHTLY ANGLED, ONTO THE REAR ROOF RACK.

B THEN LIFT THE STERN AND CAREFULLY SLIDE FORWARD.

TO LOAD FROM THE SIDE:

C LIFT THE BOW DIAGONALLY ONTO THE ROOF RACK BAR AT THE FRONT.

D THEN LIFT THE STERN ONTO THE REAR BAR, ADJUSTING IT AND SLIDING IT INTO PLACE.

left A GUIDE FROM MONKEY RIVER TOWN RESTRAINS SEA KAYAKS ON THE BACK OF A TRUCK ON A FAST RIDE TO THE RIVER BELIZE IN THE CARIBBEAN CITY OF THE SAME NAME, IN CENTRAL AMERICA.

Transporting a kayak by air

The folding kayak is the obvious choice for those who wish to paddle in faraway places. It is well worth shopping around for the best travel deal for you and your craft. Bear in mind that the cheapest option may not be the best, as careful packing and handling are vital to the safety of your kayak.

Getting your kayak to the sea

Lifting and carrying a kayak comfortably owes more to technique than to strength. The easiest method is simply to carry the kayak with a partner. This is just a matter of emptying the kayak of heavy gear and, with one person at either end, lifting it by the carrying toggles or by the ends of the kayak itself.

Carrying a kayak on your own is more of a challenge. First, empty the kayak. Find the balance point — usually a little forward of the seat — and mark the spot on either side of the cockpit coaming. Follow the instructions set out below. To lower the kayak, use the same procedure in reverse, using your knee to lower the kayak gently to the ground.

Sometimes you'll have to carry a loaded kayak, e.g. when embarking on a long expedition. The best way is for four people to carry one kayak at a time. If you have no option but to do it alone, or with one other kayaker, move the kayak along the beach by swivelling one end around 180 degrees and repeating the process with the other end.

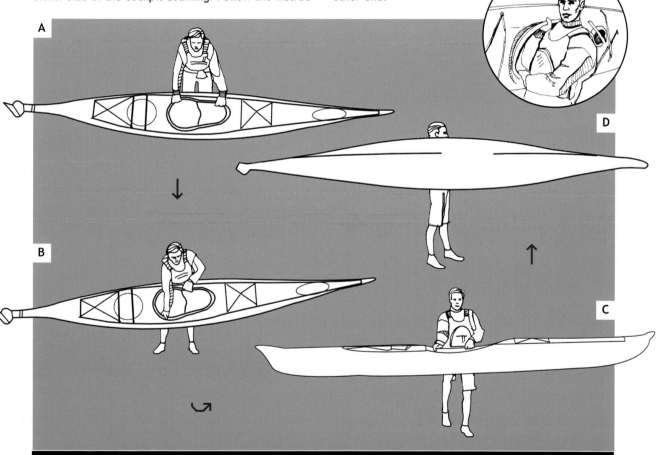

A SQUAT DOWN TO LIFT, WITH YOUR BACK AS STRAIGHT AS POSSIBLE. GRASP THE COCKPIT COAMING CLOSE TO YOU WITH YOUR HANDS EQUIDISTANT FROM THE CENTRE POINT. PULL THE KAYAK UP AGAINST YOUR LEGS, WITH ITS OPPOSITE SIDE STILL ON THE GROUND.

B STRAIGHTEN UP, RELYING ON YOUR LEGS TO LIFT THE KAYAK, THEN RAISE IT WITH YOUR ARMS.

C THE KAYAK IS NOW AT WAIST LEVEL, WHERE YOU CAN CARRY IT FOR A SHORT DISTANCE. TO GET IT ONTO YOUR SHOULDER (THE EASIEST POSITION FOR CARRYING), GET AN UNDERHAND GRIP ON THE OPPOSITE COAMING WITH ONE HAND. USE THE OTHER HAND ON THE NEAR COAMING AS A PIVOT WHILE YOU BRING THE LOWER HAND TOWARD YOU AND UP. SIMULTANEOUSLY, RAISE ONE KNEE TO LIFT THE KAYAK.

D SLIDE YOUR SHOULDER UNDER THE COCKPIT COAMING AND YOU'RE READY TO GO, USING YOUR HAND TO BALANCE THE KAYAK.

Entering and Launching the Kayak

To launch or land in calm conditions is not difficult but both paddler and kayak are most unstable during this procedure. Make sure you are wearing full kit, including the sprayskirt and PFD.

Launching from a beach

Carry your kayak to the water's edge. A sit-on sea kayak can be launched by dragging it knee-deep into the water, straddling the seat and dropping yourself down on it whilst lifting your legs into the foot wells.

Launching a sit-in kayak from the beach requires a little more effort. Try this method:

Place the kayak on the sand at the waterline, seat yourself with the paddle in one hand and secure the sprayskirt. Use your free hand and the paddle to push the kayak toward the water until it is afloat. You can use your body to help move the kayak forward by lifting yourself slightly off the seat and using your knees and feet to push forward, balancing yourself with your free hand on the sand.

Alternatively, straddle the kayak in shallow water, lower your bottom into the cockpit, then slide your feet in one by one. Wait for a lull between wave sets and launch off, paddling vigorously to get through the waves.

TO LAUNCH FROM A BEACH, ATTEMPT TO 'WALK' THE KAYAK TO A SUFFICIENT DEPTH OF WATER, AS DESCRIBED ALONGSIDE.

You could also use your paddle to stabilize your entry: let the kayak float in several centimetres of water and bring it alongside the beach. Stand in the water between kayak and beach, facing the bow. Place your paddle behind your back, with its shaft across the craft's back deck, perpendicular to the centre line. One side of the blade should rest flat on the beach, the other will be just over the side of the kayak. With the hand closest to the craft, hold the paddle shaft in a backhand grip and place the other hand further up the shaft. Without putting too much strain on the paddle, sit down on the back deck. Bring one leg in, then the other, leaning towards shore for balance. Now either lower yourself down to the seat with your knees bent; or move your legs under the deck until you can lower yourself onto the seat. Bring the paddle around and secure it, then get the sprayskirt in place.

Launching from a platform

This may be easier than from a crowded beach. You could attempt any of the three following methods:

(1) Using your paddle for balance, sit as close to the edge of the platform, or dock, as possible, facing in the same direction as the bow of the kayak. Put the paddle behind you, with the shaft across the craft's back deck, just behind the cockpit. Hold the paddle shaft against the coaming of the cockpit with one hand, and put the other on the dock. Bring in one leg at a time, lowering yourself onto the seat.

(2) Sitting on the dock edge, use your arms to lift off and swing yourself over the kayak, lowering yourself slowly into the seat, while keeping your weight on your arms until you're seated.

(3) From a squatting position near the edge of the dock, support yourself with your legs and one hand and grasp the coaming with the other. Keep your weight over the dock and swing the leg closest to the kayak into the cockpit. Swing the other leg into the craft and settle into the seat.

High docks are more difficult to enter from. Test whether it will be possible for you, by sitting on the very edge of the dock and dangling your legs over the side. If your legs are within reach of the kayak, you can continue. Leaving your paddle on the dock, where you can readily reach it from the kayak, sit on the dock's edge with your feet holding the craft in place. Twist to face the bow and roll onto your front with your lower body hanging off the dock. Lower yourself onto the seat, bending your knees as you do so. Keep your weight on your hands until you are confident that you are stable and that the kayak will not slide out from beneath you. Now sit down carefully and retrieve your paddle.

Launching from rocky coasts

Where there is little sand, this can be tricky. However, there are several ways to accomplish it: With the kayak in shallow water amongst the rocks, lay your paddle across the back deck to form a bridge between your kayak and the rock. Using the paddle for balance, sit down by sliding your legs into the kayak. Lean slightly toward the rock to prevent a capsize. Once you're seated with the sprayskirt in place, allow the kayak to float into the water by taking the weight off it with the paddle and your free hand to clear the rocks below the surface. This is known as a rock launch.

A seal launch can be made from a rocky slope or descent. Seat yourself in the kayak at a spot nearest the water, where you're able to balance it. Hold the paddle upright with one hand, pushing with the free hand to gain momentum. Keep your balance as the craft slides down into the water.

A

B

above TO EXIT YOUR KAYAK ON THE BEACH, PLACE YOUR PADDLE BEHIND YOU AS SHOWN IN **A** AND LIFT YOURSELF OUT AS ILLUSTRATED IN **B**, BEING CAREFUL NOT TO EXERT EXCESSIVE PRESSURE ON THE COCKPIT RIM, DECK OR PADDLE. FOR THE ENTRY PROCEDURE THE PROCEDURE IS SIMPLY THE SAME, IN REVERSE.

below IN ROCKY AREAS YOU CAN USE A SEAL LAUNCH TO ENTER THE WATER. POSITION YOUR KAYAK ON A SLOPING ROCK AND CAREFULLY MANOEUVRE FORWARD, STRIVING TO MAINTAIN YOUR BALANCE AS THE BOW DIPS UNDERWATER. THIS KAYAKER SHOULD BE WEARING A HELMET, PARTICULARLY AS HE IS LAUNCHING FROM ROCKS.

Launching and landing through surf

Find a spot on the beach where the waves are smaller, allowing you to launch the kayak. Position yourself in the craft, with your sprayskirt in place, right at the edge of the water, bow facing into the waves. Allow wash from the bigger waves to float the kayak. Watch the waves, gauging the duration of sets (a number of large waves, followed by some smaller ones) and the window period (the relatively calm period between sets of waves). Push off in the calm period at the end of a set and paddle strongly, directly into the waves. If a wave should break in front of you, lean forward and push

A KAYAKER HEADS IN FOR A DRY EXIT ONTO THE DOCK, LAKE WANAKA, NEW ZEALAND.

through it. Bring the paddle in under one arm and direct it through the wave to create a streamlined movement, but be ready to paddle strongly once on the other side. Don't turn your craft in front of a wave; the only way to negotiate it is to meet it head-on.

Landing in surf is more difficult than launching, as it is not easy to determine wave sets when facing the shore. Paddle as close to the shore as possible. Look and listen carefully, glancing over your shoulder to watch for incoming swells. When you think the last big wave of a set has passed, paddle vigorously to shore. Try to get to shore on the back of a gentle wave, running in behind it rather than surfing it in. Be prepared, though — you might be caught by a wave from behind that will push you to the shore. Angle the kayak to one side to slide down the face of the wave, leaning back to avoid perling (when the kayak buries its nose in the trough of a wave and you go head over tail).

You may be able to surf right up the beach, but your kayak may broach and bump along parallel to a wave. In this event, brace into the face of the wave to avoid a capsize. As soon as you touch sand, alight from the kayak and pull it by the bow, clear of the surf. Watch

for incoming waves and ensure you don't dawdle in the craft.

Landing in dumping surf — caused by a shore bottom with a steep shelf — is difficult and dangerous. Land as before but surf as far up the beach as possible. Once you touch the shore, jump out and grab the kayak to prevent it being sucked back by the next wave.

Dry exits

For a dock landing, simply manoeuvre your kayak alongside the dock and place the paddle on the dock. Shift backward in your kayak to clear your knees of the deck so that you can bend them. Squat and then stand up, supporting yourself by holding on to the dock.

Paddling in wind and surf

Once in a while the sea will be like a glassy pond, but more often than not, you'll be dealing with a variety of sea and weather conditions.

Headwinds and oncoming seas These are the easiest and safest to paddle in, and you'll feel stable and comfortable. Paddling into oncoming waves and headwinds is hard work, but keep going. Stopping not only causes you to lose the ground you've already covered, but may turn the kayak in a direction that you can't recover from. This is where a sea anchor may come in handy, as on long hauls you can set a sea anchor to allow you to take a break before continuing upwind.

Following wind and sea Travelling with the wind and sea behind one is exhilarating for a kayaker skilled enough to go with the flow. Energy is conserved by allowing wind and waves to push the craft forward. However, if the waves are large, controlling the kayak becomes a challenge and a variety of surf techniques may be called for to keep on track; novice paddlers, may become unstable and capsize. This is usually caused by the kayak's swinging round and broaching on a wave. When this occurs, the paddler must use bracing techniques to prevent capsizing.

Cross winds and beam sea In this situation, the waves and/or wind come from the side. Inexperienced paddlers may feel as if they're being blown over sideways. Even for experienced paddlers, cross winds require constant vigilance if one is to keep the kayak upright and on course. In these conditions, steady yourself with the paddle, angling the top of the backward-travelling blade towards the stern.

In large waves, use brace techniques — the high or low paddle brace (see p 49) — to maintain balance. To lessen the impact of the wind, keep a 'low profile', curling yourself down and keeping the paddle as horizontal as you can. An unorthodox technique for use in extreme conditions is to shorten your paddle on the windward side and extend it on the leeward side. This allows you to brace on every leeward stroke, but slows progress. A well-executed forward stroke can also act as a powerful brace.

Overhead winds Wind may come from directly overhead (e.g. when travelling close to a cliff and a strong wind blowing out to sea pushes downward) — you may feel you're being buffeted from all directions. Your best option is to head further offshore, where the wind is more manageable, even if the sea is rougher.

Wind for kayak sailing Wind may also be harnessed to sail a kayak. With a following wind, a sail can have a dramatic impact on speed, allowing one to conserve energy on a long trip. Some folding kayaks (such as the Klepper) have sophisticated optional sail rigs. However, a small hand-held fan sail or a makeshift sail tied to a paddle will do as well.

Dealing with waves A breaking wave takes three forms: it can plunge (dumping wave), surge up a steep beach, or spill over away from the beach in a peeling-off motion. Surging and plunging waves usually occur when the ocean swell meets a shore that has a steep sloping bottom. When the wave reaches a point where its depth is equal to its height, it will break with crushing force, making launches and landings very difficult.

Spilling waves, created by a swell approaching a gently sloping shore or reef, are easy to paddle in or out through, but can become too large to manage.

Refracting waves bend when they reach shallower waters near the shore. As the wave bends it gets smaller, making the place of refraction a good landing spot. Bays usually offer good landing places and fine swells. When a swell enters the bay, the largest surf is in the middle, and due to refraction, the wave will be smaller at the edges.

Water is also pulled back out to sea by rip tides at the sides. This helps to flatten the surf, facilitating launching and landing. Waves also refract around islands or rocky outcrops close to shore.

Clapotis occurs when an incoming swell meets an obstruction like a sea wall or cliff. Incoming swells collide with the water falling back from the barrier. Clapotis may be dangerous for paddlers, as the force of colliding water might send the kayak flying. Always pay extra attention when paddling close to the shore.

LAUNCHING AND LANDING THROUGH SURF REQUIRES PATIENCE AND GOOD TIMING. IF YOU HAVE MISJUDGED THE WAVE SETS, PADDLE STRONGLY AND PUNCH THROUGH THE WAVES, KEEPING YOUR CRAFT AT A RIGHT ANGLE TO THE WAVES AT ALL TIMES.

Paddling techniques

Paddle position

Grip the paddle equidistant from each blade, with your hands about shoulder-width apart. Holding the paddle with hands far apart makes for easier but less effective paddling. You may achieve a longer reach with your hands close together, but this will cause strain.

Gripping the paddle

The knuckles of your control hand must be in line with the top edge of the reverse blade. The paddle should be firmly but not tightly held in order to avoid blisters and strain. Opening your hands at the push stage releases strain on the arms and improves your style.

Forward stroke

It may seem obvious, but the way in which you take a stroke through the water has an impact on your ability to sustain pad-dling for any length of time. When you watch really skilled paddlers, they appear to be stroking the water effortlessly. Achieving a well-executed, smooth, economical stroke takes practice, but is worth striving for. Once you have mastered the basics, you will find the other paddle strokes follow naturally, as your confidence grows. Here are some suggestions, beginning with a simple forward stroke:

PULLING FORWARD EFFICIENTLY:

A PLACE THE BLADE IN THE WATER COMFORTABLY IN FRONT OF YOU.

B ROTATE YOUR TORSO, TRANSFERRING POWER TO THE BLADE.

C LIFT THE BLADE FROM THE WATER WHEN IT PASSES BEHIND YOUR HIP.

D WIND UP FOR THE NEXT ROTATING ACTION, KEEPING THE MOVEMENT SMOOTH AND STAYING RELAXED. ALLOW YOUR TOP HAND TO OPEN TO RELIEVE STRAIN AND TENSION. KEEP YOUR FEET FIRMLY BRACED TO TRANSMIT THE FORWARD MOTION TO YOUR KAYAK.

- Stretch out your arm and place the blade at a comfortable distance in front of you, trying to make as little splash as possible.
- Keep the blade as close to the kayak as possible, without holding the paddle upright.
- Use your whole body to pull the blade back, twisting your torso and shoulders from the waist, which engages the abdominal muscles.
- Lift the blade from the water, creating as little of a splash as possible.
- Now push the blade forward, continuing the rotation of your upper body so that your arms don't take all the strain.
- Develop a smooth stroke that comes naturally — a low stroke will conserve energy and reduce resistance to wind.

Paddle braces

These strokes help to stabilize the kayak when you feel you're losing your balance. The paddle brace is one of the most important of all sea kayaking techniques, as it keeps the paddler upright under various conditions, such as when a kayak broaches and you have to brace against a wave to avoid capsizing. These are the basics:

A low brace is performed quite simply, without altering the normal paddling position. Place the paddle on the surface of the water, with the driving face downward. Keeping your wrists straight, perform a short, firm, downward and forward push of the blade.

A high brace may be needed in big waves or when landing through surf. Lean the kayak into the breaking wave. Pull your elbows in close to your body, raising the paddle to the level of your shoulders. Dig the paddle into the wave, keeping the face of the blade turned down. Support comes from a downward pull with the face of the blade.

A sculling support stroke is based on the same principle as the sculling draw stroke (see p51). To execute this stroke, hold the paddle in either the normal or the extended paddling position. Move the paddle face down, almost flat against the surface of the water, to and fro in a small arc. This stroke will provide constant support for a stationary kayak, keeping you level on the surface of the water, or will pull you back into an upright position if you're leaning precariously to one side.

A HIGH BRACE IS USUALLY USED WHEN BRACING FORWARD OF THE CENTRE LINE, SUCH AS WHEN LEANING FORWARD AGAINST A WAVE. KEEP YOUR ELBOWS CLOSE TO YOUR BODY TO AVOID A SHOULDER DISLOCATION.

TO ACHIEVE THE BEST CONTROL OF YOUR CRAFT, ENSURE THAT YOU ARE SITTING FIRM IN YOUR SEAT. NEOPRENE STRIPS CAN BE GLUED TO THE INSIDE OF YOUR KAYAK IN THE PLACES THAT YOU BRACE AGAINST. SIT-ON KAYAKS CAN BE FITTED WITH FOOT STRAPS, KNEE BRACES AND LAP STRAPS. WHEN PADDLING IN SURF IT IS ADVISABLE TO WEAR A HELMET.

Manoeuvres with rudders and skegs

Some kayaks turn well with a rudder; others turn better without one but need a rudder to track a straight course. You need to experiment with your rudder to find out what applies in your case.

Rudders do have their limitations: if a rudder is turned too sharply, it may act as a brake. In rough seas, the blade may lift out of the water and cause you to lose directional control when it submerges again. Also, rudder cables may snap, leaving you adrift.

A skeg can help you to manoeuvre, but you need to adjust it to suit the conditions e.g. in a cross wind, the kayak will turn upwind with the skeg retracted, and downwind with it deployed.

To turn a kayak without a rudder, simply stroke harder on the side opposite to the direction in which you wish to turn. However, to make acute changes of direction — such as when avoiding rocks or assisting in a rescue — the forward and reverse sweep stroke techniques will be helpful.

THE FORWARD SWEEP STROKE IS USED TO TURN THE CRAFT. TO TURN LEFT YOU PERFORM THE STROKE ON THE RIGHT SIDE OF THE KAYAK, AND VICE-VERSA.

THE REVERSE SWEEP STROKE CAN BE USED IN CONJUNCTION WITH THE FORWARD SWEEP TO TURN THE KAYAK QUICKLY FROM A STATIONARY POSITION.

Manoeuvring strokes

The **sweep stroke** allows you to change direction or correct the direction of the kayak.

In the **forward sweep stroke**, reach forward and place the blade close to the side of the craft. Sweep the paddle outwards and then backwards with the blade submerged, moving in a semicircle. Finish the stroke with the paddle just behind you.

The **reverse sweep** (opposite of forward sweep stroke) can be used on one side and the forward sweep on the other to turn the kayak quickly while stationary.

The **stern rudder stroke**, corrects instability caused by a following sea (waves approaching from behind causing the kayak to surf forward, perhaps out of control). Place the paddle blade in

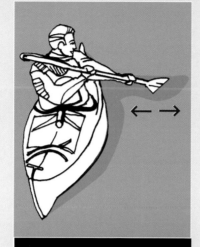

THE STERN RUDDER STROKE CAN BE USED WHILE MOVING FORWARD, AND IS ESPECIALLY USEFUL IN RUNNING SEAS TO MAKE CORRECTIONS TO YOUR COURSE.

TO MANOEUVRE YOUR KAYAK SIDEWAYS, PULL THE BLADE DIRECTLY TOWARDS YOU IN A DRAW STROKE **(A)**, OR PERFORM THE SCULLING DRAW STROKE, A FIGURE-OF-EIGHT SWEEP WITH THE BLADE **(B)**.

the water behind you, with the blade facing outward. Then, push the blade out and away from the side while the kayak is moving forward, so that it turns to that side.

The **draw stroke** (see A below) helps to position the

kayak beam-on during rescues. It may also be used to pull the kayak sideways to reach a particular point, such as a quay. Extend the paddle over the side in the direction you're aiming for, and submerge the blade vertically, keeping it at a constant depth, with the face of the blade towards the kayak. Now, pull the paddle towards you, and the craft will move towards the paddle. Repeat the action until you reach the desired position.

The **sculling draw stroke** (see manoeuvre B in illustration below) is similar, but instead of pulling the paddle toward you, move it back and forth in a figure eight, turning the driving face as you do so. The blade planes through the water in each direction, pulling the kayak towards it. This stroke can also be used to push the kayak in the opposite direction.

The draw stroke and sculling draw stroke can be invaluable in preventing a capsize, so learn them well.

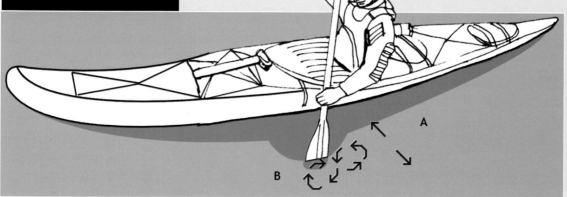

Recovery and self-rescue

'Rescue' and 'recovery' in sea kayaking terms mean nothing more dramatic than sorting yourself out after a capsize or wet exit (falling out in deep water). You may paddle many leagues without capsizing, but you must be prepared for this eventuality. Acquiring the essential skills for self-rescue and recovery makes for confidence at sea.

It is essential to practise wet exits. You must familiarize yourself with the sensation so that you're prepared for the shock of its occurring at sea. You are only able to practise re-entry techniques after a wet exit, so take the plunge and let yourself capsize!

In the case of sit-on kayaks, remounting after a capsize is a relatively simple matter of turning the craft back up by clambering over the upturned hull, gripping the opposite edge and pulling it back over with you. Then launch yourself over the seat indentation and swing one leg over the rear of the craft to straddle it, facing the bow, before swinging yourself forward into the seat and bringing your feet up into the footwells. Traditional sit-in sea kayaks require more specific techniques.

Rolling

Rolls may be perceived as functional strokes or as forms of recovery or self-rescue techniques. Previously known as Eskimo Rolls, these maneuvers were developed by the Inuit peoples as life-saving techniques for use in Arctic conditions. Sea kayaks are relatively large craft and may be heavily laden, making them cumbersome to roll in all but perfect conditions, so this is a foolproof method of recovery, but it may prove useful if you have learned to perform it correctly. You can practise in a pool with someone to help you at first.

Central to the roll is the motion of the hips. The objective is to right the kayak when it is upside down, bringing you with it. To do this you must be able to use your knees and buttocks to flick your hip up, bringing the kayak along with it. Using this rapid action of your lower body, along with the correct paddle position, creates enough momentum for the buoyancy of the kayak to bring it upright.

Screw roll This technique gets its name from the motion involved — the paddler seems to screw round and through the water, twisting her body to surface upright. Mastery of the motion rather than the strength of the paddler achieves the roll. It is quick and efficient, and the position of one's hands doesn't change from the standard paddling position.

Once upside down, get into the 'wind-up' position: hold the paddle alongside the kayak with the front blade, power face down, nearly flat on the surface. Then sweep the front blade outward along the surface until it is at an angle of 90 degrees to the kayak, which helps to bring the kayak nearly upright. Now brace downward with the paddle, and use a hip flick to right the kayak. This flick pulls your torso out of the water.

Reverse screw roll This is a variation on the above technique, in which the blade position is reversed: the outward sweep is made with the rear rather than the front blade. The reverse screw roll is used if a regular screw roll fails (similarly, a screw roll can follow a reverse screw which fails) or if the paddle has been pushed onto the back deck during the capsize.

Pawlata roll This is similar to the screw roll, except your hands change position. When you're leaning into a capsize, the forward hand holds just forward of the centre of the paddle shaft, the back hand holds the rear blade against the kayak. The front hand rotates the paddle to sweep the front blade outwards as in the screw roll. Follow through with the hip flick action, which can be more powerful than for a screw roll as the paddle offers more support. This may be the easiest roll to begin with.

Pivot roll Also known as the 'headstand', this roll requires that you change your usual grip on the paddle, as the roll depends on the resistance of the blade being forced down in the water. To practise the pivot roll, your head must be above water — a sculling brace will help achieve this. Move the paddle out until one hand is holding the nearer blade, while the other grips the shaft as far along as possible. Extending the outward blade as far as possible, pull down firmly with your outer hand; the hand on the near blade serves as a pivot. A powerful hip flick, together with the pivoting

Rolling basics

MASTERING THE BASIC ROLL will give you confidence and could prove invaluable in case of a capsize. The screw roll shown here is a popular technique.

1. Balance your kayak and relax, taking two or three deep breaths.

2. Set up the paddle as shown in the 'wind-up' position. You may prefer to hold the paddle on the opposite side of the kayak, with your right hand at the rear. Hold this position while you turn upside down.

3. Orientate yourself and set up for the sweep. You may even knock the rear blade against the craft to ensure it is raised correctly.

4. Sweep the forward blade towards the rear, keeping it initially close to the surface and then leaning on it to commence the hip flick.

5. The hip flick should turn the kayak enough for its own buoyancy to assist with the raise. Lean back; raise your head last.

6. Once up, steady yourself to avoid a re-capsize.

7. Orientate yourself. Relax and continue paddling.

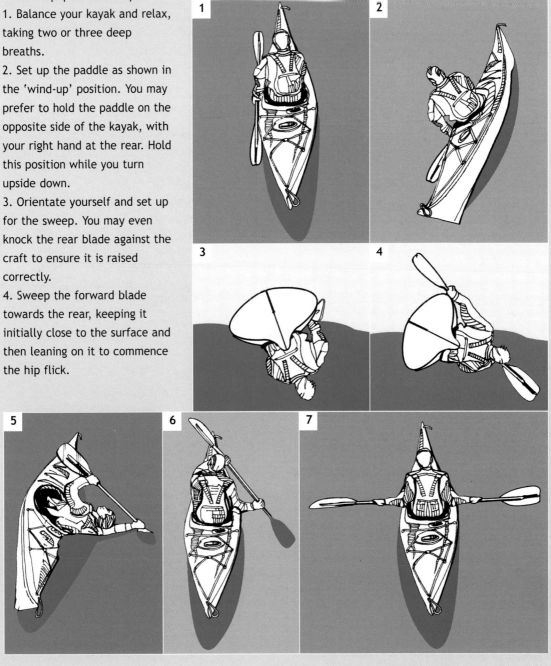

action of the paddle, will correct the kayak. Once upright, pull the paddle out of the water smartly or its resistance may roll you over again.

Remember to raise your head last in all rolls. Leaning back toward the stern also reduces water resistance against your body, and may improve your roll.

The swimming pool is an ideal place to practise the rolls. Using a diving mask permits you to see what's going on and prevent you from inhaling water. If you can find an instructor to teach you the rolls and other self-rescue techniques, so much the better.

It is always recommended that, before touring, sea kayakers practise the rolls and other self-rescue techniques with a laden kayak, which is often easier but may be a challenge for the beginner. A waveski may be used for initial practise, as it allows you to get the hang of the rolls without having to empty the craft every time you exit, but you should ideally practise in the kayak you will be using at sea.

It is advisable to wear your PFD at all times; you will find, too, that it is an aid to rolling.

Re-entry and roll

In the event of a wet exit, you'll be swimming alongside the overturned kayak you need to re-enter. If conditions permit and you are confident of your rolling technique, you can attempt to enter your kayak while it is still upside down and roll it up, saving you the effort involved in a paddle float rescue. Position yourself next to the cockpit, facing the rear of the craft. Wait for a window in the waves, take a deep breath, duck under the kayak and enter the cockpit. Lock your knees in under the deck, position your paddle and roll back up, using the roll you find easiest and most reliable. If your paddle is attached to a leash and your sprayskirt attaches easily, you may like to re-attach the sprayskirt before performing the roll. This will prevent more water entering the kayak. Once stable, bail the excess water out of the craft. A sea anchor aids stability while you pump out water. If you're with a partner, he or she can help by securing your kayak in a rafting position (side by side, with the partner holding your cockpit), while you pump.

THE ABILITY TO EFFECTIVELY ROLL YOUR CRAFT ADDS A WHOLE NEW DIMENSION TO YOUR KAYAKING PLEASURE AND SAFETY. PERFECT THE ART IN A SWIMMING POOL, PREFERABLY WITH AN EXPERIENCED INSTRUCTOR, AND BUILD UP THE CONFIDENCE TO PERFORM IT IN THE OCEAN. REMEMBER THAT ROLLS CAN FAIL AND YOU DO NEED TO HAVE A FOOLPROOF BACKUP SELF-RESCUE TECHNIQUE AT ALL TIMES. ENSURE THAT YOUR SPRAYSKIRT IS EASILY UNFASTENED FOR A QUICK EXIT FROM THE KAYAK IN AN EMERGENCY. A PADDLE LEASH ENSURES YOU DO NOT LOSE YOUR PADDLE IN AN EMERGENCY.

Other self-rescue techniques

There will be cases when you have to wet exit, possibly in deep water. If you have not successfully learned to roll, or are not confident with the technique, you may choose to wet exit in the event of a capsize. No matter what the circumstances, always maintain a firm grip on your kayak while in the water.

Using a paddle float for re-entry

After capsizing, you may use the paddle float for recovery, either to assist with a re-entry and roll or to serve as an outrigger to assist the re-entry. The first method is helpful in heavy seas; it is time-consuming to set up but, once in place, an effective roll is ensured. To make the re-entry: attach the paddle float and follow the steps for re-entry and roll outlined opposite. The float provides leverage to bring the kayak upright. Once corrected, brace the paddle across the cockpit rim — so it serves as an outrigger — keeping the kayak stable and enabling you to pump out water and regain your composure.

Paddle float outrigger re-entry

This is particularly useful in rough conditions. In extreme conditions a sea anchor or drogue may be used to keep the bow facing oncoming waves, so that the kayak does not broach as you climb back in. For this re-entry the kayak must be upright.

If it is upside down, push up on the edge of the cockpit to roll it over, or lie over the hull, gripping the far side of the cockpit rim, and pull the kayak over towards you. Once the kayak is upright, attach the paddle float and secure the paddle to the deck webbing or paddle-park. Position yourself facing the stern. With the paddle extending out on the left side of the kayak, pull yourself into the kayak by holding the paddle shaft with your left hand, the cockpit with your right hand, while pushing down on the paddle to draw the body up. Use the paddle shaft as a support for your leg while you pull yourself up over the deck of the kayak. Pull your legs in, while leaning face-down over the back deck. Slide down into the cockpit and twist around to face forward. Pump out excess water with the paddle float still in place.

Rear-mount re-entry

In certain conditions and with a kayak that has a large freeboard and cockpit, you may find it easiest to launch yourself out of the water over the stern of the kayak, straddling it. Keeping your body flat on the deck, edge forward until you can slide your legs into the cockpit and then drop your buttocks in. Many modern kayaks have quite small cockpits, which are useful for keeping water out of your craft, but can make it a little more difficult to re-enter the kayak while at sea. Sliding your legs in first should do the trick.

FOR A PADDLE FLOAT OUTRIGGER RE-ENTRY, FIRST TURN THE KAYAK UPRIGHT AND BAIL OUT EXCESS WATER IF NECESSARY. PLACE THE PADDLE BEHIND THE COCKPIT AND PULL YOURSELF OUT OF THE WATER AND OVER THE KAYAK TO THE REAR OF THE COCKPIT. PIVOT AROUND AND SLIP IN.

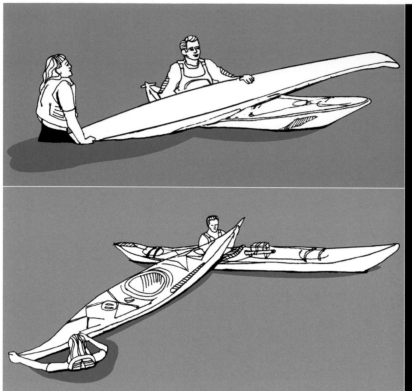

top TO EMPTY A CAPSIZED KAYAK USING THE 'T' RESCUE, THE RESCUER RAISES THE BOW OF THE SWAMPED CRAFT ON TO HIS FRONT DECK. THE PERSON IN THE WATER ASSISTS BY FIRST PUSHING DOWN ON AND THEN LIFTING THE STERN OF THE KAYAK, CREATING A ROCKING MOTION TO EMPTY THE CRAFT OF WATER. NOTE THAT THIS TECHNIQUE ONLY WORKS ON KAYAKS WITH BULKHEADS.

bottom ONCE EMPTIED OF WATER, THE CRAFT IS RIGHTED AND THE RESCUER SLIDES IT BACK INTO THE WATER, WHERE THE PADDLER CAN EFFECT A RE-ENTRY BY MEANS OF THE SIDE-BY-SIDE RESCUE TECHNIQUE. THIS TECHNIQUE IS PARTICULARLY USEFUL IF ONLY ONE RESCUER IS AVAILABLE. ALTERNATIVELY, THE 'TX' METHOD CAN BE USED IF THE CAPSIZED KAYAK IS ALMOST FULLY SWAMPED.

Assisted Rescues

In a group or with a paddling partner, there are simple and effective techniques for getting each other out of trouble when in deep water. Two or more kayaks rafted together provide far greater stability than a single craft. This is an advantage in a group rescue.

Emptying water from a swamped kayak

If a kayak has been fully swamped, the following 'curl' technique may be used to empty it. Once the craft has been brought to the surface, it is positioned upright next to the rescuer's kayak in reverse position. The paddler in the water pulls him-/herself over the front deck of the rescuer's craft from the opposite side by placing the hands, palms up, under the coaming of the cockpit of the swamped kayak. He or she then pulls the swamped kayak towards the rescuer's craft, tilting it so that water pours out. Meanwhile, the rescuer leans over in the opposite direction, effecting a sculling support stroke to help empty the kayak. When the kayak is empty, re-entry can be carried out.

Emptying a half-swamped kayak (T and TX Rescues)

These rescues also get their names from the position of the kayaks, and require only one rescuer. He or she grabs the bow of the capsized kayak and lifts it across the front deck of his/her kayak, so that the upturned craft rests near the rescuer's cockpit. The rescuer rocks the kayak by moving his/her own craft from side to side, while the paddler in the water assists by holding and lifting the stern of the kayak. The empty kayak is turned over into the water where it's held in the side-by-side rescue position for re-entry. The TX rescue is used if the kayak is almost fully swamped, in which case it is pulled further over the rescuer's craft, forming an 'X' shape, in order to empty it.

Side-by-side rescue

Once the capsized kayak has been righted, the rescuer positions his/her kayak parallel to the other kayak, bow to stern, and holds onto the rim of its cockpit. The paddler in the water can now enter from the other side, using a powerful kick to pull him- or herself onto the rear deck, facing the stern and then sliding the legs into the cockpit, and twisting around to face the bow. The rescuer secures the kayak while the rescued person attaches the sprayskirt, pumps out excess water and regains control of the kayak.

HI rescue

This technique calls for two paddlers to assist the capsized paddler:

The rescuing paddlers position their kayaks parallel to one another, facing the capsized paddler. They retrieve the paddle and hold it, along with their own paddles, across the gap between their two kayaks. The resultant formation looks like the letter H or I, hence the name 'HI' rescue.

The capsized paddler directs the bow of his or her upturned kayak between the rescue craft, and the two rescuers lift the capsized kayak swiftly over the paddles. The kayak rests, upturned, on the paddle while the rescuers hold the craft steady and rock it to empty it of water. The kayak is then turned upright, and the rescuers slide the paddles out from underneath it. Now the capsized paddler can enter the kayak while it is secured between the other two kayaks.

All-in rescues

If one kayak in a group capsizes, there's a strong possibility that others will follow, too. Several paddlers in the water may nevertheless assist with each other's rescue.

Two paddlers in the water: Each paddler rights his or her own kayak. They then position their kayaks parallel, bow to stern. One paddler swims between the kayaks, holding both cockpits, while the other enters from the outside. The paddler in the water then re-enters, assisted by a side-by-side rescue technique.

Three paddlers in the water: Paddler A holds onto a kayak (1) and looks after all the paddles (holding them between the legs, to free up his or her arms). Paddlers

B and C hold onto the cockpit of one of the other kayaks (2), and face in opposite directions. B lifts the bow of the third kayak (3) and pulls it quickly over kayak (2), so that the cockpit rests on the upturned hull. Paddlers A and B rock kayak (3) until it is empty. It is then turned upright alongside kayak (2). Paddler B positions himself next to the cockpit and re-enters, holding on to a paddle and the cockpit rim, while paddler A stabilizes the two kayaks for this re-entry. As soon as B is in the kayak, A's kayak is emptied, using the TX rescue, then C re-enters his/her kayak using the HI rescue method.

Double kayak rescues

It is not impossible to capsize in a double kayak. To effect a rescue, the paddlers co-operate to right and re-enter the kayak. The paddlers position themselves on either side of the rear cockpit; one holds the kayak steady while the other re-enters. The paddler in the kayak uses a sculling brace on one side of the craft, to allow the other paddler to re-enter from the opposite side.

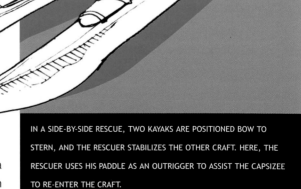

IN A SIDE-BY-SIDE RESCUE, TWO KAYAKS ARE POSITIONED BOW TO STERN, AND THE RESCUER STABILIZES THE OTHER CRAFT. HERE, THE RESCUER USES HIS PADDLE AS AN OUTRIGGER TO ASSIST THE CAPSIZEE TO RE-ENTER THE CRAFT.

Towing

Towing may be necessary if one paddler in a group is injured or exhausted. A tow line may also be used if a paddler has capsized near a dangerous coastline onto which he/she may be blown, or if a paddler finds it difficult to maintain a course in strong headwind or running sea.

If the distressed paddler is in the water, get them back into the kayak using the most efficient rescue technique. If the paddler is injured it may be necessary for a second paddler to enter the water to assist them with re-entry, although this is not recommended unless there is absolutely no other choice. Definitely do not enter the water if you are the only other paddler. In groups, it should be possible to improvise a strategy to raise a distressed paddler out of the water and into a kayak without anyone needing to enter the water. This is where double kayaks can come in particularly useful,

as the distressed paddler can swap places with one partner from a double kayak. The injured or exhausted paddler can then be paddled to safety, while his or her rescuer paddles the single kayak. If this option is not available, towing will be necessary. Use a snap shackle or tie a line to the kayak's bow toggle and fasten it to your waist using a waistband which can be released quickly. Although towlines used to be fastened to the deck of the towing kayak, advances in waistband design have made it far safer to use this method.. A third kayak with an extra tow line may be employed in front of the towing paddler, to increase the pulling strength. In case of an emergency, the tow line must have a quick-release mechanism so that the rescuer can be released from the craft being towed. It is polite to undo a towline, if possible, shortly before your destination is reached, so that the paddler can retain their dignity by paddling him or herself in to shore.

KAYAKS HAVE ENOUGH MOMENTUM TO BE EFFECTIVE TOW CRAFT, PROVIDED THE BOW TOGGLES AND TOWING POINTS ARE SUFFICIENTLY REINFORCED TO BEAR THE STRAIN. CONDITIONS WILL DICTATE THE LENGTH OF THE TOW ROPE BUT GENERALLY A SHORTER ROPE MAKES FOR EASIER TOWING. HOWEVER, A ROPE AS SHORT AS THAT SHOWN ABOVE MAY NOT ALWAYS BE FEASIBLE.

Calling for Assistance

If you are alone and in difficulty, you can use one of the emergency signalling devices discussed in Chapter 2, or use the paddle signals illustrated below if within sight of another craft. If you can not re-enter your kayak despite every effort, try to alert rescuers to your plight. How you do this depends on your location, the time of day and other factors. Most importantly:

■ Stay with your kayak at all times — it is more visible than you are. Do not leave it to swim after a paddle, since you should have a spare on the kayak anyway.

■ If close to land and you are confident that you can get there, try to swim ashore holding onto the kayak

■ Only leave the kayak if you are close to the shore and you risk being swept out to sea if you hang on to it

■ If you are forced to abandon the kayak, take your survival kit with you, preferably attached to your PFD

■ If far from land, use the VHF radio emergency channel, cellphone or other means of communication

■ If you see a vessel heading your way, fire off a meteor flare and use your signal mirror (if it is sunny). Never assume that you have been spotted; it is easy to be missed by passing craft. Continue to signal until you are sure your rescuers have seen you

■ In darkness, fire a flare and switch on your strobe

■ Use a distress banner to help aircraft to spot you

All sea kayakers should fill in a float plan for leaving ashore with a responsible person. The plan should clearly outline your destination, course and estimated time of arrival.

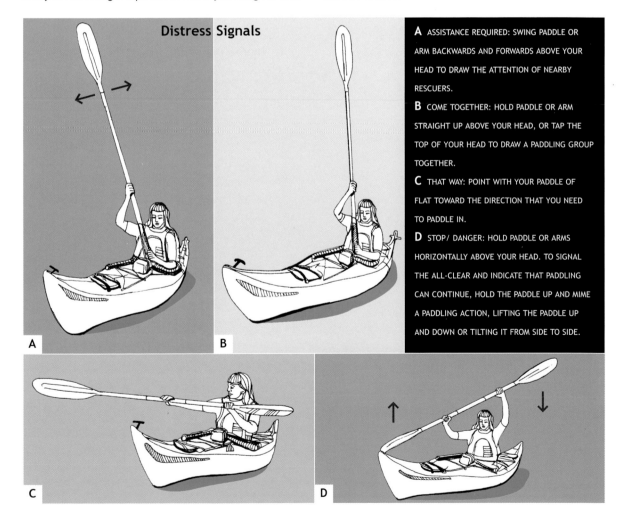

Distress Signals

A ASSISTANCE REQUIRED: SWING PADDLE OR ARM BACKWARDS AND FORWARDS ABOVE YOUR HEAD TO DRAW THE ATTENTION OF NEARBY RESCUERS.

B COME TOGETHER: HOLD PADDLE OR ARM STRAIGHT UP ABOVE YOUR HEAD, OR TAP THE TOP OF YOUR HEAD TO DRAW A PADDLING GROUP TOGETHER.

C THAT WAY: POINT WITH YOUR PADDLE OF FLAT TOWARD THE DIRECTION THAT YOU NEED TO PADDLE IN.

D STOP/ DANGER: HOLD PADDLE OR ARMS HORIZONTALLY ABOVE YOUR HEAD. TO SIGNAL THE ALL-CLEAR AND INDICATE THAT PADDLING CAN CONTINUE, HOLD THE PADDLE UP AND MIME A PADDLING ACTION, LIFTING THE PADDLE UP AND DOWN OR TILTING IT FROM SIDE TO SIDE.

A

B

C

D

Seamanship and Navigation

Sea kayaking can be a great adventure. In your lightweight, eco-friendly craft, you can reach some of the most isolated parts of the world, see spectacular fauna and flora, and have a close-up view of the wonderful diversity of marine life. Before you paddle off into the sunset, however, you need to know more about the sea: how to read it and how to find your way around it. True seamanship comes of years of experience, but the essential guidelines offered here provide a useful starting point.

Grading sea conditions

Every time you go for a paddle on the sea you have to decide whether it's safe to do so. Your decision will depend on your reading of sea conditions, including weather, tides, winds and waves. Some of these you can see for yourself, but don't disregard weather reports, barometer readings and other available technologies. Combine all the factors and grade the conditions according to a 7-point scale, from 'easy' through 'fair' to 'not on your life'! Then honestly assess your abilities and you'll have an indication of whether you can paddle in safety. Grading changes according to the prevailing conditions. However, some static features, such as whether the route lies in a protected bay, whether you are going to be launching and landing in the same place and whether the area has rescue services, will contribute to its grading.

above THE OPEN OCEAN MAY BE DAUNTING FOR THE UNPREPARED, BUT FOR THOSE WHO HAVE ACQUIRED THE ESSENTIAL SKILLS AND KNOWLEDGE, IT CAN BE THE MOST EXHILARATING PLACE ON EARTH.

opposite IF KAYAKERS CORRECTLY USE THEIR KNOWLEDGE OF THE WEATHER AND TIDES, THEY CAN SAFELY EXPLORE DANGEROUS AREAS OF COASTLINE. IT IS VITAL TO HAVE THE NECESSARY SKILLS AND CONFIDENCE BEFORE PADDLING IN SUCH CONDITIONS.

Tides and currents

An understanding of how tides work, and how to read tide and tidal current tables, is a prerequisite skill of seamanship. Knowing how to predict tides and currents, even without tables (for you may travel to isolated areas where none are available), is an indispensable skill for sea paddlers.

Tides are the result of the daily rise and fall in sea level, originating from the 'bulge' of water that occurs as a result of the moon's pull on the earth. The bulge follows the moon, which explains the variation of the daily and monthly tides.

Spring tides, a higher high tide and lower low tide than usual, occur during new moon and full moon. At new moon, both the moon and sun are on the same side of the earth, creating a strong pull and increasing the size of the bulge (see illustration below). At full moon, the moon and sun are on opposite sides, creating an oppositional pull which also increases the size of the bulge and consequently the height of the tide. Because of the lie of land masses and the inertia of the body of water, the bulges usually occur one or two days after the calendar dates for full and new moons.

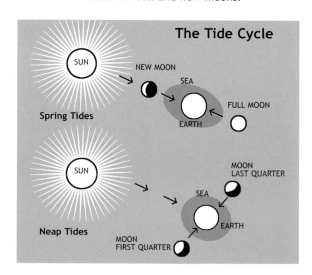

The Tide Cycle

ANNUAL TIDAL CHARTS ARE USEFUL TO KAYAKERS PREPARING DAILY TRIPS. THEY INDICATE WHEN HIGH AND LOW TIDE WILL OCCUR ON ANY GIVEN DAY. FROM THESE THE DIRECTION OF TIDAL STREAMS CAN BE DETERMINED. NOTE THAT ADJUSTMENTS WILL HAVE TO BE MADE ACCORDING TO HOW FAR AWAY YOU ARE FROM THE LOCATION UPON WHICH THE TABLE IS BASED AND ALSO WHETHER YOU ARE DEALING WITH RESTRICTED WATER FLOW AREAS LIKE LAGOONS. TIDES WILL AFFECT YOUR LAUNCHES AND LANDINGS IN AREAS SUCH AS THAT SHOWN ABOVE. AT LOW TIDE SMALL RIP CURRENTS OR GULLIES MAY BECOME EXPOSED, MAKING PADDLING FROM HERE POSSIBLE. AT HIGH TIDE ROLLERS FORD THE BARRIERS AND COME IN UNRESTRICTED, MAKING LAUNCHES AND LANDINGS ARDUOUS AT THE LEAST.

Neap tides, which show the least difference between high and low tides, occur during the first and last quarter of the moon. The pull is weaker because the sun and the moon pull at right angles to each other, thus dissipating their effect (see illustration on p 60).

There are usually two high tides and two low tides daily, occurring within six hours of each other. However, in some regions of the world only one high and one low tide occur each day. In some places tidal differences may be small, in others they may vary greatly, causing tidal races.

Tide charts are important to your trip, as they indicate times and heights for tides in the area and help you predict tidal currents. Remember that the predicted heights and times of tides may be affected by winds and atmospheric pressure. Low pressure increases tidal range, high pressure moderates it. It is useful to learn to read the phases of the moon and watch the water to predict tidal conditions on those occasions when no tables are available. Knowledge of the so-called 'perpetual tide table' for your area will give you an indication of the tides if you know which phase the moon is in.

Tidal streams are more significant to kayakers than the vertical rise and fall of the tides. They usually occur near land, especially in areas where tides are forced through narrow straits. Streams are said to be in flood or ebb depending on whether the tide is high (flood) or low (ebb). When either tide reaches its limit, there is a calm period called 'slack water'.

In a rapid stream, you will need to time your crossing to the slack water period. In relatively gentle tidal conditions, you can take advantage of the stream if it's flowing in the right direction. If it's working against you, try to find the eddy streams near the shore which sometimes flow in the opposite direction to the main tidal stream.

Tidal streams flow at different speeds depending on the quarter of the tide. The speed of tidal streams is related to the speed in which the tides rise or fall. In order to work out how fast the tide rises (and therefore how fast tidal streams are flowing), you can use the rule of twelfths:

- the first hour after low tide: tide rises 1/12 of its total height
- the second hour: tide rises 2/12
- the third hour: tide rises 3/12
- the fourth hour: tide rises 3/12
- the fifth hour: tide rises 2/12
- the sixth hour: tide rises 1/12

Tidal streams flow fastest in the middle two hours between high and low tide. The rule of twelfths gives an indication of the depth of the water at a particular time in the tide. To calculate the actual speed of the tidal flow, it is necessary to know its maximum speed (supplied in some tide tables, nautical charts or almanacs). The rule of 50/90 then applies and works like this:

- decide whether the tides are on spring or on neap (neap speeds are assumed to be half that of spring)
- one hour after a tide turns, it moves at 50% of its maximum speed
- two hours after the tide turns, it moves at 90% of capacity
- after 3 hours it is moving at maximum speed
- the same process applies in reverse after 3 hours, going down to 90% and then to 50%

Charts will usually indicate dangerous tidal streams, such as those that cause whirlpools or large waves. Areas to beware of with respect to tidal streams include narrow passages between land masses, like those between islands or between an island and the mainland. Careful navigation is required for such crossings, drawing on the navigation chart as well as the tide tables to establish the right time and place to make a crossing. If streams cannot be avoided, the ferrying technique is a good ploy; paddle into the tidal stream at an acute angle, to minimize its effect (see illustration on p 70).

Tidal streams are also affected by the contours of the sea bottom and by wind. Wind moving in the direction opposite to that of the stream can create dangerously large waves.

AT LOW TIDE, AND IN GENTLE SEAS SUCH AS THAT SHOWN ABOVE, LAUNCHES AND LANDINGS ON THE BEACH, AND PADDLING DIRECTLY OUT THROUGH THE SURF, WILL BE RELATIVELY EASY.

Waves

Offshore winds (blowing from land to sea) or onshore winds (blowing from sea to land) create different wave conditions. The profile of a wave is defined by:

- the crest: its highest point
- the trough: the depression between two waves
- the height: the difference in height between crest and trough
- the length: the distance between two wave crests
- the fetch: total distance over which waves can build

The formation of different land masses creates different wave conditions. Waves reflect, refract or bend:

- a wave hitting a sea wall or cliff will 'reflect' from it, creating clapotis, dangerous for paddlers
- waves refract around islands, creating rough water and clapotis on the far side of the island
- waves entering a bay refract around the headlands and bend as they approach the shore, creating manageable surf conditions inside the bay
- waves are variable and sets differ so they require constant monitoring while one paddles through them

A kayaker's seamanship is demonstrated by his or her judgement of waves and the ability to launch and land efficiently through surf, contributing to versatility.

above A DEMANDING STRETCH OF COAST WITH A WIDE FETCH; A BIG SWELL AND LARGE WAVES; VARIABLE LENGTHS BETWEEN WAVES; A COMBINATION OF SPILLING AND DUMPING WAVES; AND STRONG RIP CURRENTS, WHICH ARE BOTH USEFUL AND TREACHEROUS. THIS STRETCH COULD BE GRADED 6 OR 7, AND WOULD REQUIRE SKILL TO NEGOTIATE IN A SEA KAYAK. IT IS NOT RECOMMENDED FOR RECREATIONAL TRIPPERS!

below IT IS USEFUL TO KNOW THE DESCRIPTIVE TERMINOLOGY FOR THE DIFFERENT FEATURES OF A WAVE, GIVING PADDLERS AN UNDERSTANDING OF HOW THE WAVE WORKS, AND ALLOWING THEM TO PLAN HOW BEST TO NEGOTIATE IT.

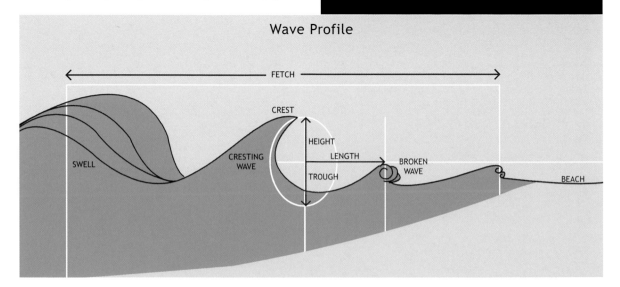

Wave Profile

FETCH

CREST

HEIGHT

LENGTH

SWELL

CRESTING WAVE

TROUGH

BROKEN WAVE

BEACH

Weather

Weather reports have made it easier to plan for a kayaking trip, but a sound understanding of how the weather can shift will stand you in good stead. An assessment of local conditions, combined with some knowledge of weather patterns for an area, is necessary if one is to make credible predictions.

Developing weather awareness and strategy When planning a trip to a particular place at a particular time, one must gather as much detail as possible on the typical and atypical climatic conditions for that area at that time of year. Pay attention to any likelihood of strong winds and storms during your proposed trip. Once in the area, obtain local information on the weather and sea conditions for the location you plan to paddle in. Also, check radio weather reports as regularly as possible.

Before a major crossing Carry out hourly and daily checks of sea, sky, wind and cloud conditions. A hand-held anemometer will give accurate readings of wind velocity, which will clearly indicate whether it is safe to paddle. Clouds also help to predict future weather trends (e.g. high cirrus cloud usually predicts the approach of low pressure, and therefore bad weather, within a day or two).

Use your barometer to verify predictions: generally, rising atmospheric pressure predicts fine conditions, falling pressure indicates approaching bad weather. If the pressure drops rapidly, a storm is probable. In temperate zones, long steady rises generally predict fine weather that will last, while a sudden rise could mean the weather will turn. Modern digital barometers, which include a 24-hour display of pressure, temperature and humidity, are useful.

Be sensitive to atypical weather conditions for the season and area as warnings of a turn in the weather. Observe insects and animals, which seem to sense the approach of bad weather. When a storm threatens, terns become more active than usual, seagulls gather on shore, insects abound, seals are more playful, and dolphins may leap from the water, dropping back with a loud smack.

Learn to use whatever is at hand, from weather reports to electronic equipment and natural phenomena, to assess weather conditions. That way you'll be able to grade conditions with accuracy, and ensure that you make the right decision about the planned trip. Nevertheless, you should always take the proper precautions and have an escape plan ready should your prediction go awry.

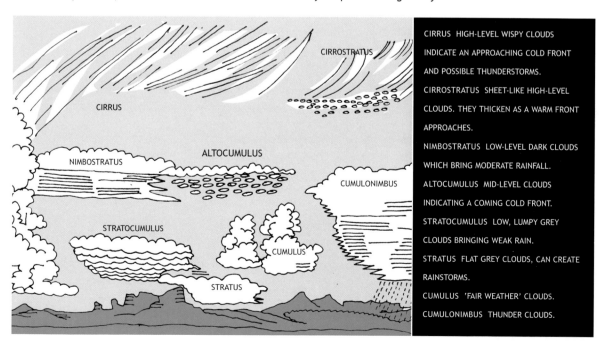

CIRRUS HIGH-LEVEL WISPY CLOUDS INDICATE AN APPROACHING COLD FRONT AND POSSIBLE THUNDERSTORMS.

CIRROSTRATUS SHEET-LIKE HIGH-LEVEL CLOUDS. THEY THICKEN AS A WARM FRONT APPROACHES.

NIMBOSTRATUS LOW-LEVEL DARK CLOUDS WHICH BRING MODERATE RAINFALL.

ALTOCUMULUS MID-LEVEL CLOUDS INDICATING A COMING COLD FRONT.

STRATOCUMULUS LOW, LUMPY GREY CLOUDS BRINGING WEAK RAIN.

STRATUS FLAT GREY CLOUDS, CAN CREATE RAINSTORMS.

CUMULUS 'FAIR WEATHER' CLOUDS.

CUMULONIMBUS THUNDER CLOUDS.

Navigation

Navigation is the art and science of steering your craft on a desired course and calculating your position at sea. If you are travelling a coastal route, the advantage of being able to see land makes it more unlikely that you will get lost. Nonetheless, navigation is essential to any tour on the ocean. To navigate a kayak, the following equipment is essential: nautical charts, a compass, a watch, dividers (or a piece of string with

distances marked on it), a courser or ruler and protractor, and notes on your readings of weather and sea. Good navigation requires constant vigilance of your approximate location, confirmed by whatever method is available to you. Even on a coastal route, you need to predict accurately what lies ahead, and plan for landings.

Charts

To make sense of a nautical chart, it is useful to know how the science of navigation works. Cartographers have created a grid of imaginary 'lines' covering the earth — the lines of latitude and longitude — in order to make it possible to read your location. Lines of latitude (use 'flatitude' as a memory aid) are horizontal lines parallel to one another and to the equator, the central reference point at 0°. Lines of longitude, also known as meridians, run vertically north to south, converging at the poles. Given that there is no natural reference point for these lines, Greenwich Observatory in the United Kingdom was chosen to mark 0° of longitude.

Each degree of latitude and longitude is further divided into 60 minutes and then 60 seconds. To describe a position on the globe, latitude (indicating location north or south of the equator) is stated first, followed by longitude (which indicates degrees east or west of the Greenwich meridian).

A nautical chart will also have these lines inscribed across the map, with degrees indicated in the margin. It is a detailed map of the ocean, and covers:

- depth of water
- speed and direction of streams
- seabed topography
- navigational aids (buoys, beacons, etc.)
- coastal features and configuration

It is essential to navigation that you have some practical knowledge of charts, how to read them and how to plot a course using one. The legend on the chart will explain which system is used for the measurements, e.g. metres, feet or fathoms.

Magnetic Variation vs True North

UNFORTUNATELY FOR SEAFARERS, MAGNETIC NORTH, THE NORTHERLY DIRECTION INDICATED BY A COMPASS, IS NOT THE SAME AS TRUE NORTH. THE VARIATION BETWEEN THE TWO DIFFERS FROM PLACE TO PLACE AND CHANGES OVER TIME. NAVIGATORS MUST WORK THE CORRECT VARIATION INTO THEIR CALCULATIONS WHEN PLOTTING OR FOLLOWING A COURSE FROM A CHART.

The compass rose will indicate the north/ south/ east/west direction, giving true north as well as magnetic north, which needs to be adjusted for variation within a specific area. The legend will also indicate scale (the ratio of what is shown on the chart to reality). A nautical chart symbol index, available from marine shops, will explain the symbols used. Suitable charts for sea kayaking range from 1:50,000 to 1:150,000,000. For detailed exploratory trips, choose the larger scale.

It's a good idea to cut or fold the chart into squares which are then individually laminated. You will need to have a compass rose copied on to each individual section of the chart in the appropriate position. With an erasable marker, plot a course on the plastic-coated chart. Keep the chart in a transparent map bag secured to the kayak; you can't afford to lose it.

Plotting a route

First, using a rule, draw a course line from your starting point to your destination. Use the dividers to measure the distance by spreading them until the points are at the start and end of the course, then place them on the distance scale. In this way you can calculate how many nautical (or land) miles you have to paddle (1 nautical mile = 1.15 land miles, which is approximately 1.6km). If no scale is provided, use the latitude scale on the side of the chart in which 1 min = 1 nautical mile). Mark off nautical miles along the latitude scale of the chart on a piece of string and measure distance with that. Don't use the longitude scale along the bottom of the chart for this purpose.

The compass rose on your chart indicates the direction of true and magnetic north. From the north–south direction on your chart, you can use a hand-held compass to get a bearing for your route and end destination. Instructions on how to use the compass are provided later in this chapter.

Having plotted a course and started paddling, check your distance against the clock so that you know how fast you're going and how long it should take to get to your destination. To measure speed, mariners use knots: 1 knot is 1 nautical mile per hour (or the

equivalent of about 1.15 land miles/1.6km). With experience you'll learn how to use your chart effectively to get an overall picture of an area and recognize the challenges it may present.

LEARNING TO NAVIGATE USING NAUTICAL CHARTS AND A COMPASS WILL ADD A NEW DIMENSION TO YOUR SEA KAYAKING EXPERIENCE AND IS ESSENTIAL IF YOU PLAN TO TAKE LONG TRIPS IN UNFAMILIAR AREAS. CUTTING LARGE CHARTS INTO INDIVIDUALLY LAMINATED SQUARES (PREFERABLY NUMBERED SO THAT YOU KNOW WHICH PIECE GOES WHERE) WILL MAKE IT EASIER TO CONSULT YOUR CHART WHILE AT SEA. LAMINATION ALSO MAKES THE CHART A LITTLE FIRMER AGAINST THE WIND, AND PROTECTS IT FROM THE WATER.

Compass

Once you have plotted your route on a chart, you can hold the course with the aid of a compass. On the compass, north is 0°, east is 90°, south is 180°, and west is 270°. So, if a point is directly to the south of you, it is said to have a bearing of 180°.

To comprehend the difference between a magnetic bearing and a true bearing, one must know that the arrow on the chart that points north indicates the geographic North Pole (true north). The north-pointing needle on the compass indicates magnetic north (a variation caused by the earth's magnetic field, which moves slowly over the years). The difference between true north and magnetic north is acknowledged on charts and needs to be calculated for accurate navigation — this difference is known as 'variation' on a nautical chart and 'declination' on a topographical map. All charts will list variation for the area, as it differs from place to place.

If you are navigating with a chart, you'll need to work out the compass bearing by adjusting for variation. If the magnetic variation is east, simply rotate the compass so the needle points to the indicated variation and your 0° mark will now indicate true north. If the variation is west, you will have to subtract the variation from 360°. Some compasses will have an adjustable variation arrow which can be set to orient it to true north.)

To take a true bearing, set the variation of the hand-held compass to the local variation. Now, hold the compass in front of you so that the 0° is aligned to true north. While holding the compass directed towards the destination, move the compass dial until the needle is aligned with the variation arrow. Read the number on the degree dial which matches the direction for which you're aiming, and you have a true bearing.

To take a chart bearing, draw a straight line from your present position to your desired position. Place the compass so that its edge and the directional arrow follow the line of your course. Turn the dial until the north lines on the face align with the north lines on the chart. The degree mark on the compass dial that aligns with the direction-of-travel line on the base of the compass is the true bearing. Alternatively, set the dial in line with the magnetic compass rose on the chart to get a magnetic bearing.

As you gain experience, you will be able to use the process of mental dead reckoning, calculating as you proceed how far you have come along your desired course. This involves paying attention to landmarks along the way, calculating drift while paddling, and remaining constantly aware of changes in weather and paddling speed.

Global Positioning System (GPS)

The GPS consists of a pocket-sized waterproof computer that relies on satellites to fix a position. It provides information on speed, distance travelled and distance remaining, among other things. GPS's have become popular with hikers and are now standard equipment for sail- and powerboats. This micro-navigation system is ideally suited to sea kayaking, and with the advance of technology, should become standard equipment on touring kayaks. If you choose to use a GPS, it is still essential to be familiar with the skills of chart navigation and compass reading in case of an electronic failure or flat batteries.

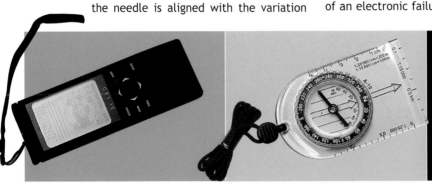

left A HAND-HELD COMPASS OR GPS (FAR LEFT) CAN HELP YOU TO OBTAIN AND KEEP YOUR BEARINGS WHILE PLOTTING OR TRAVELLING A ROUTE. A SMALL COMPASS SHOULD ALWAYS ACCOMPANY YOU, THOUGH, IN THE CASE OF BATTERY OR ELECTRONIC FAILURE OF THE GPS.

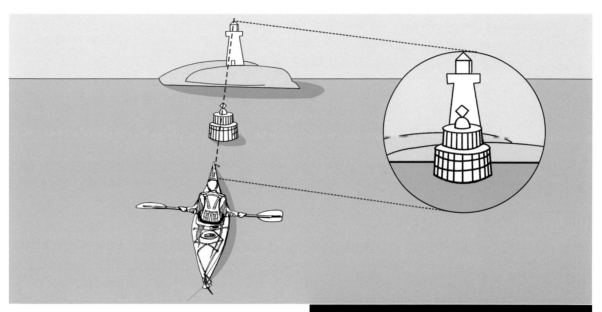

Transits

Another navigation technique makes use of 'transits', or leading marks. This simply means keeping two land-marks (e.g. lighthouses, hills, buildings on land) aligned, ensuring that you're able to hold a course. Choose two highly visible, stationary marks — ahead or abaft — and paddle to a point where they're in line with each other. Paddle on, ensuring that they're always aligned; this will keep you to a straight course and thus following the desired route. If one object moves left or right of the other, it means you are off course and must paddle in the opposite direction to correct your course.

This method is particularly useful when ferrying against a tidal stream or a cross wind to confirm that your ferry angle is correct and that you are moving towards your destination. It's useful to check forward progress by checking the crossing of transits abeam of you. Objects may also be aligned to fix the positions of points of interest, such as reefs and wrecks, at sea. By lining them up and remembering the transits, you'll be able to locate them again later.

If you wish to fix their positions on a chart, transits may be connected with a line that is projected out to sea. Your position lies at the intersection of two or three such lines. If you can't line up objects, the bear-

> BY ALIGNING OBJECTS ON THE SHORE YOU CAN STAY ON A PREDE-TERMINED COURSE, LOCATE A PLACE OF INTEREST, OR DETERMINE YOUR POSITION ON A CHART. NOTING HOW THE OBJECTS MOVE APART CAN GIVE YOU AN ACCURATE INDICATION OF YOUR DRIFT AND SPEED. ALTER YOUR PADDLING DIRECTION IN ACCORDANCE WITH THESE SIGNS IN ORDER TO MAINTAIN YOUR COURSE.

ings of objects which you can locate on the chart may be taken with a hand-bearing compass, and their bearings intersected on a chart. The position to be fixed lies at the point where the bearings intersect.

Buoyage

If you are going to paddle frequently in high-traffic areas of open sea, you should be familiar with the systems of buoyage that are used to control sea traffic in restricted areas. These may include:

■ lateral marks
■ isolated danger marks
■ safe water marks
■ channel separation marks
■ cardinal marks

Make sure you know what these look like in daylight and at night (i.e. colour of lights and flashing sequences).

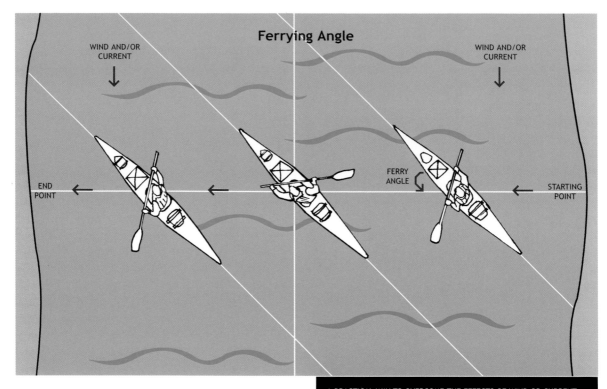

Ferrying Angle

WIND AND/OR CURRENT

WIND AND/OR CURRENT

END POINT

FERRY ANGLE

STARTING POINT

Difficult navigation situations

The following situations may present some challenges to your navigational skills.

Crossings

Crossing major channels will involve using your navigation skills in conjunction with your knowledge of weather, shipping, hazards, etc. When making such a crossing, keep an eye on your progress: keep track of your location and the time, and bear in mind the influence exerted by high and low tides.

Tidal streams

Channels often have tidal streams which impede or accelerate your progress. Careful timing, based on tide tables and chart readings, will help you to avoid streams (or, where this is not possible, to deal with it as best you can). You won't always be able to avoid the stream, given the length of some crossings. If this is the case, use the ferrying technique, paddling at an angle to the stream or wind to minimize its impact on your desired course (see illustration above).

A PRACTICAL WAY TO OVERCOME THE EFFECTS OF WIND OR CURRENT ON YOUR COURSE IS TO SET A FERRY ANGLE TOWARDS A TARGET UPWIND OR UPCURRENT OF YOUR DESIRED DESTINATION. PADDLE FOR THAT POINT, USING TRANSITS IF POSSIBLE TO MAINTAIN YOUR BEARING. WHEN CLOSE TO THE OVERSHOOT POINT, YOU CAN RELAX A LITTLE AND ALLOW THE PREVAILING WIND OR CURRENT TO CARRY YOU TO YOUR DESIRED DESTINATION.

You can use common sense to establish an approximate ferrying angle or you can calculate the correct angle by drawing a diagram and juxtaposing your speed of travel with the speed of the stream. The most practical solution is to aim to overshoot your target when setting your ferrying angle. Knowing that the stream of wind will push you, for example, south of your target, you aim well north of it, selecting a landmark to help you keep your bearing. If you have underestimated the distance and the effects of the elements, adjust your ferrying angle when it becomes apparent that you are going to be swept south of your target. When approaching the overshot point, enjoy a downwind or stream-assisted run to your desired destination.

Wind

Wind has a marked impact on a kayak, so make use of all your navigational strategies to minimize its effects. Keep a vigilant eye on what the wind is doing and how it may affect you. To compensate for winds that may blow you off course, use the ferrying technique described opposite. Avoid making crossings in headwinds which exceed 20 knots, as you'll make little progress.

When kayaking along windy coastal regions, you'll either be paddling along a lee shore (where the wind is blowing on to land) or a windward shore (with the wind blowing off the land), so you need to be aware of the conditions which may prevail in either situation. Lee shores can be dangerous, with heavy surf. Plan to arrive at these in daylight and navigate towards the most protected spot. The advantage of lee shores for kayakers is that wind and streams are more liable to sweep you on to land, rather than out to sea.

Windward shores, however, are usually more welcoming. The water is calmer and you should be able to clearly see rocks and other obstacles to your safe landing. If you wish to land on a small island, choose the windward shore. In some cases, though, windward shores may be buffeted by such a strong offshore wind that it makes landing impossible. Bear in mind, also, the danger of your being blown out to sea, where conditions may be very rough indeed.

Fog

Paddling in fog is dangerous, so be prepared. Paddle as close as possible to shore, keeping away from rocky areas, to keep out of range of larger vessels. Carry a whistle or foghorn to use if you hear a boat approaching, and listen for significant sounds — your sense of hearing is a vital asset in treacherous, foggy conditions. Familiarize yourself with the various audible fog signals used in the area, such as the siren, the horn and the whistle. Some paddlers recommend a radar reflector to make your kayak visible to a ship's radar, but this must be mounted high above the water, so it's not really practical on a kayak. (Others suggest using a ball of aluminium foil to create a detectable 'hot spot' inside the hull, but do not rely on this, as it is fallible.)

DESPITE YOUR BEST WEATHER PREDICTIONS, YOU MAY BE FACED WITH THE SUDDEN ONSET OF ADVERSE WEATHER CONDITIONS. THE KEY TO COPING WITH THESE SITUATIONS IS PREPARATION. HAVE A PLAN READY TO COPE WITH WIND AND FOG, AND MAKE SURE YOU HAVE ALL THE ESSENTIAL SAFETY GEAR TO HAND. EXPERIENCE AT SEA IS YOUR NEXT BEST ASSET: THE PADDLER ABOVE HAS THE STRENGTH AND TECHNIQUE TO COPE WITH ADVERSE CONDITIONS.

Rules of the road

The two most important rules to remember are:

(1) Keep right of oncoming craft

(2) Give way to craft approaching from starboard.

Generally, sea kayakers should steer clear of all craft and never demand right of way. At best, a kayak is only partially visible, so err on the side of safety and never assume you have been spotted by another vessel.

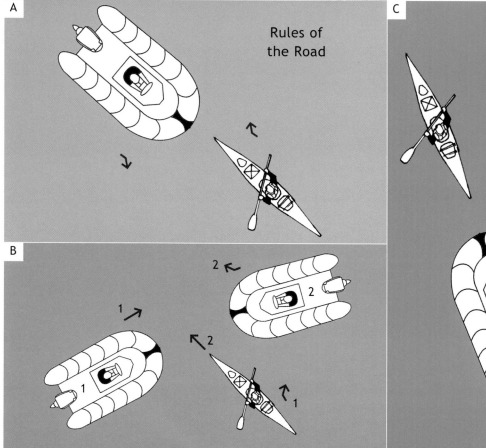

above HEAD-ON APPROACH (A): BOTH VESSELS MOVE TO THE RIGHT SO THAT THEY PASS ON EACH OTHER'S PORT (LEFT) SIDE.

SIDE-ON APPROACH (B): CRAFT 1 STANDS ON (MAINTAINING COURSE AND SPEED). KAYAK GIVES WAY (STOPS, SLOWS OR TURNS TO STARBOARD [RIGHT]),

OR: CRAFT 2 GIVES WAY TO KAYAK BY STOPPING, SLOWING OR TURNING TO STARBOARD (RIGHT). KAYAK STANDS ON.

OVERTAKING (C): KAYAK MAINTAINS SPEED AND COURSE, OTHER CRAFT PASSES TO STARBOARD.

top KAYAKERS SHOULD ALWAYS ACT DEFENSIVELY WHEN FACING LARGE CRAFT, NEVER ASSUMING THAT THEY HAVE BEEN SPOTTED.

Night paddling

Paddling at night is a magical experience if it can be accomplished safely, but is not recommended in unfamiliar areas unless the moon is full or the coast is well lit. Legislation in some countries prevents small vessels being at sea after sunset or before sunrise, probably because they lack navigational lights. Where permissible, it's best to do your first night trip as part of a group, in familiar territory and calm conditions. Make sure you're visible by carrying a headlamp and a torch, and by attaching 'glow sticks' (cyalumes) to yourself or the kayak. A head torch is handy for reading the chart or compass.

Keep a sharp ear out for approaching craft, the build-up of waves, and so on, and stay in constant verbal contact with the group. It is unwise to cross areas of heavy traffic, like busy channels, in darkness. If there is no choice but to do so, familiarize yourself with local buoyage systems. Should you encounter large craft such as a ship, the ship's lights will guide you as to its direction of travel: red on the port side (left); green on starboard (right); white at the centre of the masthead. Bear in mind that it is difficult to judge the distance of lights at night. Use your radio for further information. Most of all, be responsible and remain alert at all times.

A GROUP OF KAYAKS STANDS READY AT THE WATER'S EDGE FOR A COMMERCIAL NIGHT TOUR IN WAITEMATA HARBOUR, NEW ZEALAND. ALL ARE FITTED WITH REAR MOUNTED LIGHT STICKS TO ENSURE THAT THEY ARE VISIBLE TO OTHER CRAFT. THE PADDLERS WILL CARRY TORCHES AND WEAR HEADLAMPS.

Planning a Trip

If you choose to make your first long trip a commercially organized sea kayak tour, a lot of the planning will be taken care of, but you should nevertheless prepare adequately. Even if you don't intend to ever take a long trip, many useful tips can be gained from the kind of preplanning they require.

Before embarking on an international tour, preplan your transport, accommodation and medical care. One of the many medical assistant services currently available is Global Emergency Medical Services at Internet address www.globalems.com, which offers a 24-hour medical help desk hotline and a provider network in 190 countries. Similar services can be obtained from International SOS Assistance at www.intsos.com and Docs Online, a directory of medical practitioners, at the internet address www.docsonline.com

If you, your partners or children have medical conditions which must be noted, the MedicAlert Foundation International offers identification bracelets and a 24-hour hotline at www.medicalert.org, which provides your medical history to doctors worldwide when you are not able to.

Choosing a sea kayaking operator

If you decide to use a commercial sea kayaking operation, check whether:

■ It is an established company with a track record of reliability and safety.

■ It is registered with an association or is recommended by a tourism bureau.

■ It has professional guides and personnel, the levels of difficulty match your needs and it offers what you require — or that you understand exactly what it offers

■ Times and dates are exactly determined and the cancellation clause is understood.

■ A waiver or personal liability insurance is in place.

One of the most comprehensive worldwide sea kayaking operations is the Norwegian Canoe Association's World of Canoeing, who have an excellent site at www.woc.playak.com, while dedicated sea kayaking magazines such as US-based *Canoe & Kayak Magazine* at address www.canoekayak.com and *Sea Kayaker* at www.seakayakermag.com are useful sources of information. You can also obtain information from outdoor adventure magazines, or through tourist information bureaus, travel agencies and outdoor trade shows.

Planning an expedition

Planning a trip meticulously is the key to its eventual success. Three important issues need to be looked at. Firstly, plan your route and your schedule, using your charts, tide tables and weather information, as well as any other information on the area you will be travelling in. Secondly, give thought to what to pack for various conditions, and how to pack it. Thirdly, prepare well, both mentally and physically.

Researching a route

Once you've decided on a destination, collect all the data you can about it. Maps and guidebooks can be a source of background information on the destination and may have specific details as to the route you've chosen. Get a good topographical map of the area; it will be helpful if you decide to hike inland to areas of interest.

above SEA KAYAK SAFARIS ALONG THE COAST OF NAMIBIA, ONE OF THE LEAST POPULATED AREAS IN THE WORLD, REQUIRE THOROUGH PREPARATION AND PLANNING, AS DESCRIBED IN THIS CHAPTER.

right TRAVELLING IN A GROUP ON A WELL PLANNED EXPEDITION CAN BE AN EXCITING AND RELAXING EXPERIENCE. HERE, A GROUP OF KAYAKS IS PULLED UP WELL ABOVE THE WATERLINE IN PREPARATION FOR SETTING UP CAMP WHILE TOURING THE ISLANDS OF HAWAII.

Acquire a chart of the exact location of your route to plot it and familiarize yourself with the sea conditions, including currents and obstacles. Confirm what rescue services are available. You will also need a tide table and some knowledge of local weather conditions.

Plotting the route

Using your detailed chart, plot a route that takes into account sea and weather conditions. Although you need to be flexible, it is helpful to draw up a prospective daily paddle plan. Your time will probably be limited, so plan accordingly. Work out the total distance you'll be covering, as well as the average distance per day. Don't set yourself a heavy schedule; you'll want to enjoy the beauty of your new surroundings. About 20–30km (10–20 miles) per day is comfortable to paddle.

Make provision for unexpected events or weather conditions, and give yourself time to explore, by adding a generous allowance of extra days. This is especially important if you're flying to your destination and are therefore dependent on flight times and possible schedule changes. Time pressures can ruin a trip, and may prove dangerous if you brave difficult conditions for the sake of catching a plane.

In setting out your route, identify alternative, emergency routes on difficult passages. If it's a long journey, remember you'll need to stop to pick up provisions. A journey to foreign lands means passing through borders, so ensure that you have the necessary travel visas, shipping documents and permits.

Once there, make contact with local safety authorities and meet with them to check your route and paddle plan. If they have a good rescue infrastructure, give them a copy of your float plan with details of your route, full names and descriptions of all the members of your group and their kayaks. Include names and addresses of all next of kin. List your supplies, especially your safety equipment, and if possible arrange for check-in times via radio or cellphone.

USING MAPS AND CHARTS TO PLAN YOUR ROUTE BEFORE STARTING OUT IS ESSENTIAL. WHEN WORKING IN A GROUP IT IS A GOOD IDEA TO CONSULT ON THE ROUTE AND MAKE SURE EVERYONE KNOWS IT. HERE, A GROUP OF PADDLERS PLAN THEIR ROUTE FROM UVINJE ISLAND, OFF PEMBE ISLAND, TANZANIA

DRY BAGS WILL PROTECT YOUR EQUIPMENT AND ESSENTIAL ITEMS SUCH AS FOOD AND CLOTHING. COLOUR-CODING MAKES PACKING EASIER.

Ecologically-friendly kayaking

Paddlers are lucky to travel through unspoilt areas and are committed to maintaining their pristine state. Kayaking is itself a low-impact type of travel, but paddlers might have a negative impact unless they monitor their actions on land and at sea. Ecological sensitivity is the approach to take. The following basic precautions will ensure that you leave your camp site as beautiful as you found it:

- do not pitch tents on sensitive vegetation or dunes
- do not disturb nesting birds or animals, and ensure that your camp isn't en route to a waterhole
- do not trample on or remove natural vegetation
- do not leave litter (bury biodegradable waste)
- do not feed wild animals; it compromises the food chain
- do not use detergents for washing up; scrub with sand or salt and rinse in the sea or river
- with regard to personal ablutions: bury waste under sand or soil or use the facilities provided
- remove all traces of your presence

It adds to the fun of your tour if you lay on a few land-based luxuries. Perhaps book accommodation for a few of the nights. Or, have friends follow you on land to meet up with you at pre-arranged spots in the evening. Such arrangements also ease the burden of setting up camp and cooking night after night, and are especially welcoming after a long, hard day paddling.

Camping Gear

The bulk of your gear will be camping equipment, so consider what will be kayak-friendly. A kayak can comfortably carry about 50—100kg (110—220 lb) of gear in calm waters, and about half that in rougher seas.

Night shelter A well-designed, easy to erect, light, strong tent is essential. Even in a warm area, you'll need shelter from insects and animals. There are essentially two contemporary styles for tents: the dome and the tunnel. Domes are spacious and easy to erect, tunnels take up less storage space. Both stand up well to weather if properly designed and erected. Aluminium poles are generally better able to withstand high winds. Before buying a tent, research the market.

An awning is not essential but adds comfort, providing extra shelter from sun, rain and wind.

Bedding Essentials are a sleeping bag and mattress. Your choice of sleeping bag will be influenced by the expected weather conditions. The backpacker's thin roll-up foam sleeping mat is an option but is not as comfortable as an inflatable mattress. The open-cell foam pad offers comfort but is bulky. Inflatable designs are excellent but are vulnerable to overinflation, blowouts and punctures, so pack the repair kit!

Cooking equipment You won't resent the weight of cooking equipment when you sit down to a delicious hot meal. Most of the cooking can be done on a barbecue but a light gas stove is handy for boiling a kettle.

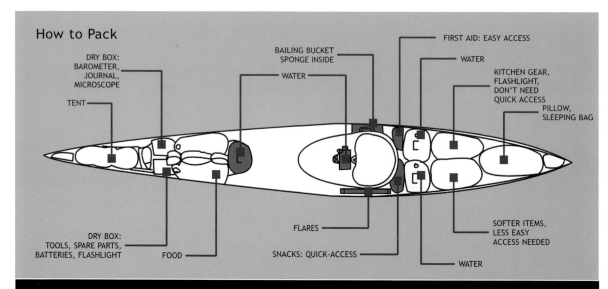

How to Pack

DRY BOX: BAROMETER, JOURNAL, MICROSCOPE

TENT

BAILING BUCKET SPONGE INSIDE

WATER

FIRST AID: EASY ACCESS

WATER

KITCHEN GEAR, FLASHLIGHT, DON'T NEED QUICK ACCESS

PILLOW, SLEEPING BAG

DRY BOX: TOOLS, SPARE PARTS, BATTERIES, FLASHLIGHT

FOOD

FLARES

SNACKS: QUICK-ACCESS

SOFTER ITEMS, LESS EASY ACCESS NEEDED

WATER

THIS DIAGRAM ILLUSTRATES HOW ALL THE GEAR YOU NEED CAN BE PACKED IN A MANNER WHICH PROPERLY BALANCES THE KAYAK AND ALLOWS FOR EASY RETRIEVAL. QUICK-ACCESS ITEMS ARE SHOWN IN PURPLE. YOUR SPARE PADDLE SHOULD BE STOWED ON DECK, FIRMLY SECURED BUT READILY AVAILABLE.

Gas stoves may be fuelled by liquid petroleum or canisters of butane/propane-type gas. Make sure you carry spare canisters. Note: take flight regulations into account; many a camper has been made to ditch -precious gas canisters or inflammable liquids.

On the utility side, you will need pots, pans and eating utensils. Nesting-pot kits are space-savers. Remember chopping boards, sharp knives, egg flippers, wooden spoons, and enough cutlery for cooking and eating. Plastic 'crockery' is light, durable and easy to clean.

Lighting The best torches are the compact, waterproof ones designed for divers. Don't forget spare batteries! Head lamps are useful when you need your hands free for cooking or pitching tents at night. For general camp site lighting, gas and electric lanterns are available in neat designs. A wind-up torch is bulky but efficient and doesn't need batteries. At a push its mechanism can also be used to charge other apparatus such as cellphones and marine radios.

Ablution equipment This may be a luxury for some, but don't underestimate the pleasure to be had from a fold-up, portable shower after a long day's paddle, especially one with simple built-in solar heating panels. Portable toilets are available, but a small spade for eco-friendly ablutions still useful.

Navigation gear Standard gear — including compass, barometer, charts, and binoculars — is essential. Store maps, charts and important papers in durable plastic-wrap or zip-lock bags.

Safety gear Make sure that you have the right safety gear for the trip. This includes signalling devices, flotation gear, sea anchor, knives and extra rope for towing.

Medical aid The basic first aid kit was described in Chapter Two. Check stocks and, for an extended tour, add extra items such as: sufficient basic medicines, plasters, and precautionary medical supplies relevant to your specific area (anti-malarial tablets in high-risk regions). Anti-diarrhoea medication and oral rehydration packs are essential, particularly for remote areas. It is a good idea to attend a first aid refresher course before embarking on an extended trip.

Survival kit In the unlikely event of having to abandon your kayak and swim ashore, it is best to pack a kit with the basics for survival until you are rescued. These should be packed in a waterproof bag, which can be easily reached, preferably attached to your PFD. The contents of this kit must include: water, food, a change of clothing, medical equipment, signalling devices, a knife, things to make a fire with, fishing kit, and your passport and other personal documents.

Packing Tips

- Avoid items that waste space (hard-sided boxes which are half-full)
- Pack for balance — making sure the kayak is balanced side-to-side, front and back
- Heavy items go at the bottom, towards the middle of the kayak
- Everything must be wedged in place; items that shift may unbalance the kayak, so pack spaces with dry bags
- Pre-empt leaks by packing everything in dry bags; sleeping in wet bedding is miserable!
- Water-sensitive items (cellphone or GPS) must have their own dry bags
- Don't risk punctures by packing sharp objects near the hull
- Pack only a minimum of gear on deck; it will make the kayak unstable and slow you down
- Safety items must be readily accessible

Packing the kayak

Follow your inventory as you pack, so essentials aren't left at home. Pack logically — for example, you won't require a tent till evening, so it needn't be immediately accessible. Snacks, however, should be close at hand! Mark things with tags or colours to identify them. Repackage food items to save space, and make preparation easier. To simplify the retrieval and repacking process, make a diagram of the packing layout (see illustration below) and stash it somewhere safe — you'll be glad you did. Do the final pack close to water; you won't want to carry a loaded kayak too far.

Food and water

The amounts of food and water you will need depend upon the length of your journey, the availability of supplies en route, and naturally, the weather. An adequate supply of potable water is essential. For all your water requirements — drinking, cooking, cleaning — you'll need to have upward of 4.5 litres (1gal) a day,

WHILST SEA KAYAKS GENERALLY HAVE AMPLE LOADING CAPACITY, BEAR IN MIND THAT YOU WILL HAVE TO PADDLE LONG DISTANCES, POSSIBLY IN INCLEMENT WEATHER. ADDITIONAL WEIGHT ALTERS THE TRIM AND CONSEQUENTLY THE PERFORMANCE OF A KAYAK. TAKE THIS INTO ACCOUNT, AND TRY TO PRACTISE PADDLING WITH A LOADED KAYAK BEFORE YOUR TRIP. SAFETY CONSIDERATIONS SHOULD ALWAYS BE FOREMOST IN PLANNING.

which can be carried in the kayak in collapsible plastic water containers. If you are relying on water from sources on land, boil it or take along a water-filtering system. Water from wilderness areas may be contaminated, so watch what you drink as an upset stomach will ruin your trip.

Don't underestimate how much food you will eat. You need fuel for heavy-duty paddling. Kayaking will sharpen your appetite, as will the fresh sea air and stimulating surroundings. In choosing food, consider dehydrated lightweight foods, especially carbohydrates like rice, pasta and soya. Fresh foods are important for their vitamin content. Not all vegetables travel well but potatoes, onions, cabbage, carrots, butternut, squash, green beans, sweet peppers, apples, and oranges are good travellers. One-pot meals comprising protein and carbohydrates, like stew, are ideal. Take healthy snacks like nuts, raisins, crackers and biscuits for instant energy. Don't forget the oil, sugar, salt, spices, coffee and tea.

SET UP CAMP IN ESTABLISHED OR PREVIOUSLY USED SITES, ENSURING THAT YOUR TENTS, EQUIPMENT AND KAYAKS ARE WELL ABOVE THE HIGH WATER MARK. FOLLOW THE GUIDELINES FOR ECO-FRIENDLY CAMPING OUTLINED ON PAGE 77, PARTICULARLY WITH REGARD TO PROPER RESPECT FOR MARINE AND LAND ANIMALS AT ALL TIMES.

Camping

Creating a comfortable camp so you can rest your weary body at the end of the day makes the trip more enjoyable. Working efficiently to a plan, you can achieve an orderly set-up quite quickly.

Setting up the camp site Preselect your camp site while planning the trip. Once there, set up camp properly to ensure a relaxing stay:

■ the kayaks and gear should be secured as far beyond the high water mark as is feasible
■ the camp must not be too far from the high tide mark, but absolutely out of range of the tide
■ once on high ground, find a flat spot for the tents
■ work briskly; don't get caught out by fading light
■ secure tents well, and be prepared for any changes in the weather
■ organize the camp properly, even just for one night
■ erect tents so that they're protected from the elements, but benefit from the view
■ consider environmental elements: is any type of animal likely to invade the site? Place things accordingly!

Cooking outdoors With the right stores and some organization, you'll truly enjoy cooking in a beautiful natural setting. For practicality, set your stove on a

ledge or rock so you don't have to bend over it. Try to incorporate local produce in your menus — fresh fish and vegetables from the market, or do your own fishing. This will also help to conserve your supplies. Share the chores so that tensions and resentments don't arise. Perhaps pairs might take turns to do chores.

Enjoy the environment Camping isn't just about eating and sleeping, it allows you the freedom to explore your surroundings. On an overnight camp, perhaps plan a walk. When you are fixing your schedule, allow time for a few forays.

A trip isn't just for kayaking and exploring on water, it's also for relaxation in a new environment. Pack a good book, take field glasses for birding, a mask and flippers for snorkelling, or a fly-fishing rod. A topographical map will be useful for land-based expeditions. A whole world is waiting out there for the intrepid sea kayaker, so take advantage of this exhilarating mode of transport to explore new environments.

Working as a group

It is important to settle on the smoothest way to work as a group. While groups will generally establish their own relationships and rules, there are some points to bear in mind:

Individual differences can have a devastating impact on a trip, so try to pre-empt clashes. Get the group together beforehand to discuss a suitable working plan.

It helps to appoint a skipper — someone who's an experienced kayaker — to make decisions. This becomes vital in dangerous situations where democracy is a disadvantage. The group must feel comfortable with the decision-maker and the leader must be relaxed and communicative in his or her management style.

Members of a group should agree on how closely together they should paddle. Keeping each other within earshot or within sight of hand signals is a good idea. In case the group becomes scattered, agree on a plan of action to regroup. This may include predetermined rendezvous points, staying in contact through radio or telephone, beaching, or returning to the last point at which they were together. Before departing, form subgroups with leaders for each; it is easier for two or three persons to co-operate than a large group. On guided tours, an experienced guide will lead and another experienced paddler will usually patrol the rear.

Paddling the route

Organize a daily paddling routine, try to stick to your schedule, but be flexible. You need to be responsive to local conditions and change plans when necessary. At the start of each day, use your original plan to indicate how far you should travel. Decide on a potential camping site before you set off. Choose sheltered spots like inlets, river mouths or islands. However, don't be rigid — if you find a perfect bay on the way and you've paddled enough for that day, simply stop. Also map out places to take lunch or other breaks. Plan for adequate breaks and allow for difficult stretches of paddling. Ensure that everybody in the group is familiar with the day's plan and arranged meeting places.

IT IS ESSENTIAL THAT A GROUP WORKS WELL TOGETHER TO MAINTAIN SAFETY STANDARDS AND ENSURE THAT THE TRIP IS FUN FOR ALL. IT IS ADVISABLE THAT THE GROUP APPOINT A LEADER OR SKIPPER — AN EXPERIENCED KAYAKER — TO MAKE DECISIONS.

Dealing with adversity

Travel is prone to problems and difficulties so make sure you know how to look after yourself. The following are some of the hazards you may face on your journey, and some tips on dealing with them.

Perils of the sea

Anyone setting out to sea in a craft needs to maintain a healthy respect for the ocean and all of its moods.

■ Research or reconnoitre launching and landing places, and have alternative plans ready

■ Take cognizance of swells and surf size, and recognize your limitations

■ Study your charts for tidal currents and rip tides: these become dangerous when misjudged

■ Beware of dangerous waves and currents which lurk in lagoon and river mouths

■ When entering a river mouth, hug the coast, staying in the shallow water on either side of the entrance

■ Coral reefs present hazards to kayaks. If they can't be avoided, cross them at high water

Marine animals

Humans are often more of a threat to animals than they are to us. Nevertheless, one is vulnerable in a kayak. It is thrilling to come close to a whale, or watch dolphins and seals frolicking, but wild creatures must always be regarded with respect. Whales have been known to charge kayakers in areas like Baja, Mexico, where they breed, and should be viewed with caution, particularly when accompanied by young.

Dolphins are a source of enjoyment to kayakers but must not be disturbed. Seals and sea lions are not aggressive but bulls may become irritated by paddlers approaching their colonies. Walruses are known to attack, often without provocation.

It is advisable to avoid shark-infested waters, but if you must travel through them, do so with due caution. In the event of a capsize, re-enter your kayak as swiftly as possible with the minimum of splashing.

Keep your distance if snakes cross your path. They might strike when confronted on open water, or board craft with a low freeboard. If you want a close-up view of marine wildlife, rather buy waterproof binoculars!

A RECREATIONAL KAYAKER STEERS CLEAR OF A PACK OF AWE-INSPIRING ORCAS AS THEY SURFACE IN FRONT OF THE KAYAK. PADDLERS MUST KEEP THEIR DISTANCE UNDER SUCH CIRCUMSTANCES, AND RESPECT MARINE WILDLIFE, NO MATTER HOW ENTHRALLING SUCH A CLOSE ENCOUNTER MAY BE.

Shipping traffic

As a paddler, one is on the lowest rung of the shipping hierarchy and kayakers should refrain from asserting their right of way. At least one sea kayaking association even recommends flying the 'D' flag, which warns other craft to 'Keep Clear!' Kayakers are unlikely to be carrying radar reflectors and would not be picked up by large ships, so it is a good idea to keep out of their way. Powerboats cause problems for kayakers, because of their speed and invasiveness. If a powerboat is hurtling towards you, your best bet is to wave a paddle as a warning of your presence. If a collision is unavoidable, roll the kayak over and try not to surface until the danger has passed. To avoid a collision, take note of the following points:

- Use visible equipment, bright clothes and PFD
- Be vigilant when entering a busy channel
- In areas of dense traffic, stay out of shipping lanes
- In fog, listen acutely to sounds and carry a fog horn
- Cross big shipping lanes only as part of a group — never alone!
- If kayaking at night, carry a torch or headlight, and the mandatory white light
- Fly the 'D' Flag

above EVERY KAYAKER SHOULD PROPERLY OBSERVE THE RULES OF SEA TRAFFIC, PARTICULARLY WHEN PADDLING IN THE BUSY LANES USED BY FISHING BOATS AND LARGER CRAFT. KAYAKERS SHOULD NEVER ASSUME RIGHT OF WAY, AND KEEPING CONSTANT VIGILANCE IS ESSENTIAL TO THEIR PERSONAL SAFETY.

below AT LEAST ONE SEA KAYAKING ASSOCIATION RECOMMENDS FLYING THE 'D-FLAG', WHICH WARNS OTHER WATER TRAFFIC TO KEEP CLEAR. ALTHOUGH KAYAKERS DO NOT HAVE RIGHT OF WAY IN SEA TRAFFIC, THE 'D'-FLAG COULD HELP TO DRAW ATTENTION TO THEIR LOW-LYING CRAFT, AVOIDING COLLISIONS.

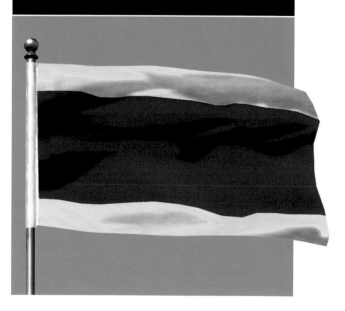

WELL PREPARED KAYAKERS WITH A SENSE OF ADVENTURE ARE ABLE TO VENTURE INTO EVEN THE MOST INACCESSIBLE AREAS AND EXPERIENCE THE
SPECTACULAR BEAUTY OF NATURE AT FIRST HAND. IT IS ESSENTIAL TO BE WELL PREPARED FOR ALL POSSIBILITIES, ESPECIALLY IN EXTREME CONDITIONS.

Injury and ill-health

What follows are some of the common injuries and ill-
nesses suffered by kayakers, and how to treat them.

Muscle and skin conditions

Tenosynovitis is a painful swelling of the tendons in the
forearm and wrist, which can happen to even the most
experienced paddlers in adverse conditions. Preventive
measures include using unfeathered paddles and/or
those with narrow blades. Remember to make a slow
start to your journey and don't drive yourself beyond
your abilities. Change your paddle grip often; don't grip
too tightly and keep wrists parallel to forearms when
paddling. Control the paddle with the lower hand.
Treatment modalities, if prevention has failed, include
anti-inflammatory medication and rest; firm bandaging
offers relief if you must carry on paddling. Massage,
acupuncture, and other remedies may be helpful.

Kayaker's Arm, a numbness in the hand, wrist or
arm, is a chronic form of Tenosynovitis which may call
for surgery. Kayaker's Elbow is a type of 'tennis elbow',
a painful inflammation caused by too much paddling or
poor technique. Shoulder dislocation is fairly common
in paddlers, especially in rough surf.

Skin conditions can make paddling very uncomfort-
able, specially chafing and rashes which may develop
through exercise and exposure to sun and salt water. To
prevent skin irritation, areas vulnerable to chafing
(such as under arms, and where the body touches the
cockpit) should be carefully rinsed of salt and sand,
and oil or petroleum jelly (Vaseline) applied. Avoid synthetic garments wherever possible. Blisters can develop on hands or feet; bandage them for protection.
Boils may arise on points exposed to pressure like the
back, buttocks, and knees. Treat with sulphur-based
creams. If this fails, resort to oral antibiotics.

Hypothermia

Hypothermia is caused by exposure to cold, when the body temperature starts to fall below its norm of around 37°C (98.6°F). No longer having the energy to keep the temperature at a steady level, the body automatically reduces blood flow to its external regions in an effort to protect the vital organs. The stages of hypothermia, in order of deterioration, include: uncontrollable shivering; rigid muscles and slurred speech; loss of brain function (memory lapse, incoherence); drowsiness; then unconsciousness, followed by death. Loss of brain function occurs after a 3°C (5°F) drop in body temperature. Prevention is therefore vital.

When paddling in cold areas, always wear warm, protective clothing and a hat, and set off on a full stomach, as inadequate nutrition, which can in turn lead to exhaustion, are two factors contributing to hypothermia. The treatment for this ailment depends on what you have available. If you're wet and cold, get warm quickly, change into dry clothes and have a hot drink. Observe fellow paddlers for signs of hypothermia like apathy or shivering, as people may not recognize the first signs themselves. Note the following:

■ Use a polyethylene exposure bag to keep the chilled sea kayaker warm
■ When carrying the victim, keep the head lower than the feet to keep blood circulating to the brain
■ Get the victim out of the cold and into warm shelter as soon as possible

In the shelter, remove wet clothing and warm the person fast. An effective method is for one or two stripped bodies to lie closely on either side of the patient, who should be placed in a dry sleeping bag. The patient can also be wrapped in a space blanket. When the person is warm, apply compresses to the head, neck, sides, chest and groin.

Administer warm, sweet drinks only when the body temperature has returned to normal. In the same vein, if sudden intense heat — such as a hot water bottle — is applied to the patient, it could cause that person to go into shock, so avoid this method.

Sunburn

Paddlers are especially susceptible to sun damage, and serious sunburn may cause blistering and dehydration. Extreme overexposure to sun may result in sunstroke, in which high fever develops and the patient may become delirious. Take precautions to prevent sunburn by applying high-factor sun protection creams generously, even on overcast days and re-applying after swimming. Always wear a wide-brimmed hat; long-sleeved clothes will shield your arms from the sun.

For extreme sunburn, start treatment by giving the patient plenty of water to drink while cooling him or her with ice packs or wet compresses. If these measures don't seem to help, get professional assistance. Long-term exposure to the sun may predispose you to skin cancer, particularly if you have a fair skin and/or a family history of such conditions.

HYPOTHERMIA CAN EASILY SET IN WHEN A PADDLER CAPSIZES IN COLD WATERS. WHEN THE PADDLER HAS BEEN RETURNED TO HIS OR HER KAYAK, THEY SHOULD LAND AS SOON AS POSSIBLE FOR TREATMENT.

Hyperthermia

A paddler may be vulnerable to this in very hot areas if the body is overheated and insufficient liquid taken in. The symptoms are a high fever, dry mouth, dizziness and light-headedness, breathlessness, distorted vision and headaches, leading to delirium and, if untreated, death. To prevent hyperthermia, always drink plenty of liquids and avoid overexertion in the heat of the day by taking a break at midday. The treatment involves cooling the body down: wet clothing, a lukewarm bath or sponging of the head, neck and wrists all help. Drinking liquids as soon as possible is also important.

Dehydration

This results from sunburn, hyperthermia or over-exertion without adequate fluid intake. To prevent dehydration, always drink plenty of liquids regularly. The barest minimum is half a litre (1pt) per day. As soon as dehydration becomes apparent, drink plenty of water laced with appropriate rehydration tablets to restore electrolyte balance. Kidney stones are a not uncommon consequence of prolonged dehydration. In this event, immediate evacuation and medical treatment are necessary.

Survival techniques

A positive attitude and a firm belief in your own abilities is central to survival — perseverance pays off. Before you take an extended tour, brush up on life-saving techniques such as mouth-to-mouth resuscitation, CPR (cardiopulmonary resuscitation), and how to deal with hypothermia, hyperthermia and dehydration. Read up on safety, rescue and survival techniques.

Survival without your kayak

If you are able to locate your emergency dry bag before losing your kayak, a dry suit with warm under-garments or a wet suit is essential, especially in cold seas. Keep your head and neck covered with a neoprene hood or woollen hat, if possible. Swim to shore if you can. If not, roll yourself into a ball and move as little as possible to preserve energy.

THESE KAYAKERS ARE ENJOYING SOME RECREATIONAL FISHING IN BEAUTIFUL SURROUNDINGS. IT IS USEFUL TO SUPPLEMENT YOUR FOOD SUPPLIES BY VISITING A NEARBY FOOD MARKET, OR CATCHING FISH AND SHELLFISH. MAKE SURE YOU CHECK ON ANY RESTRICTIONS ON FISHING IN THE AREA. THIS WILL ENABLE YOU TO CONSERVE YOUR NON-PERISHABLE FOOD STUFFS AND SAMPLE FRESH LOCAL FARE.

Lost at sea

If you have lost your bearings or are unable to reach your destination in good time, study the charts, weigh up your options and decide on a course of action. Attempt to make communication or attract attention, and try to stay positive and focus on survival. To conserve your strength, use a sail rig if the wind will take you in the right direction. Ration food and water (try to collect any rain water that falls), as it may take time to reach your destination or to get help. Consider possible food sources: start gathering seafood by setting up a fishing line if you have the materials.

Lost on land

If you're marooned on an island or in an isolated spot, display SOS using rocks or driftwood on the beach and try any means to make contact with potential rescuers. Water is a priority, so look for a fresh water source, use water purifying tablets, or try to desalinate sea water. Search for possible food sources: try fishing, hunting or collecting shellfish. Set up a shelter for protection from the sun or the cold.

Kayak repairs at sea

A repair kit is essential to your equipment. For example, your kayak may develop a leak on the open sea, forcing you to make temporary repairs there. If travelling with a partner the procedure is fairly easy.

Bring your kayak alongside that of your partner, but facing the opposite direction. Climb onto the undamaged kayak and straddle it, facing your companion. The damaged kayak may now be pulled over the other kayak, perpendicular to it, and between the two paddlers. One person secures the kayak while the other makes the repair. For the most part, repairing a leak at sea will need no more than duct tape. First clean and dry the area around the leak. Then tear off a piece of tape and apply it carefully. Squeeze out bubbles, starting at one end and rolling the strip down. Then rub firmly with a smooth object over the tape and around the corners, to prevent peeling.

In addition to the repair kit items listed below, on long expeditions fibreglass cloth, resin and latex gloves

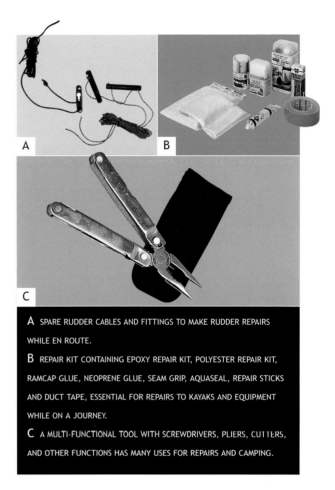

A SPARE RUDDER CABLES AND FITTINGS TO MAKE RUDDER REPAIRS WHILE EN ROUTE.

B REPAIR KIT CONTAINING EPOXY REPAIR KIT, POLYESTER REPAIR KIT, RAMCAP GLUE, NEOPRENE GLUE, SEAM GRIP, AQUASEAL, REPAIR STICKS AND DUCT TAPE, ESSENTIAL FOR REPAIRS TO KAYAKS AND EQUIPMENT WHILE ON A JOURNEY.

C A MULTI-FUNCTIONAL TOOL WITH SCREWDRIVERS, PLIERS, CUTTERS, AND OTHER FUNCTIONS HAS MANY USES FOR REPAIRS AND CAMPING.

will be needed for potential repairs to fibreglass kayaks. It is worthwhile to invest in a good book with extensive advice on kayak repair, so that even the amateur can safely make repairs as necessary.

Essential items for a repair kit are:
- screwdrivers, including jeweller's screwdrivers
- adjustable wrench
- pliers
- wire-cutters
- duct and electrical tape
- spare rudder cables and fittings
- sewing kit
- nylon cord
- all-purpose adhesive
- razor blades
- a good quality knife or 'multiple tool' on a lanyard
- silicon for waterproof repairs

World Kayaking Destinations

the following is a careful selection of some of the better known, and perhaps more frequented, sites around the world for keen sea kayakers.

Canada and USA

Sea kayaking is a popular traditional pastime in Canada. The Saguenay Fjord in Quebec (southeast Canada) offers an exciting route that takes a number of days to paddle, while in west Canada, the west coast of British Columbia is a well-known sea kayaking area, offering beautiful, wildlife-rich destinations. And the Queen Charlotte Islands, off the upper British Colombia coast, with their dramatic cliffs and over 100 islands, are regarded by many as the choice sea kayaking destination.

For kayaking in glacier conditions, the pristine wilderness of southeastern Alaska, starting at Sitka, is a popular choice.

In the USA, the north and northwest coasts are the most popular areas for sea kayaking, and are home to vast numbers of sea kayaking schools, based mainly in Seattle and Washington. One of the best trails in the country, the 483km (300-mile) Cascadia Marine Trail stretches from Olympia, Washington, to Point Roberts at the Canadian border.

The northeastern coastline, though less popular, also offers good sea kayaking. The Maine Island Trail is an exciting destination with over 4020km (2500 miles) of coves, bays and harbours. More remote adventures can be had in the Bay of Fundy and Fundy Isles.

The remote north shore of the Pacific island state of Hawaii, Molokai, is renowned not only for its world famous surfski race, but also for its exceptional recreational paddling past sheer cliffs and spilling waterfalls in a warm, tropical climate.

Florida, the Everglades and the Ten Thousand Islands along the southeast coast of the USA, as well as the coastline from Charleston to Savannah, are also good for sea kayaking, while undisturbed areas like Cape Hatteras National Seashore and Chesapeake Bay offer excellent paddling opportunities.

Central and South America

Mainland central American countries bordering the western limits of the Caribbean Sea, such as Mexico, Belize, Honduras, and Costa Rica, have inviting coastlines for kayaking and the nearby tropical Caribbean islands offer paddling on calm, azure seas.

Patagonia, a region in Argentina and Chile stretching from the Andes to the Atlantic, attracts hardy sea kayakers to some exhilarating paddling.

above THE WARM WATERS OF HAWAII ARE POPULAR WITH SEA KAYAKERS.

right THE QUEEN CHARLOTTE ISLANDS IN CANADA ARE A WELL-KNOWN DESTINATION FOR EXPLORERS IN SEA KAYAKS.

opposite THE INTREPID SEA KAYAKER CAN EXPLORE NATURE'S REMARKABLE BEAUTY IN SOME OF THE WORLD'S MORE REMOTE DESTINATIONS SUCH AS THE GRAND WALL IN THE SEA OF CORTEZ, SOUTH AMERICA.

above A GROUP OF INTREPID EXPLORERS ON A SEA KAYAK EXPEDITION AMONG THE ICE FLOES OFF ANGMAGGSALIK ISLAND, EAST GREENLAND. DESPITE THE COLD AND THE DIFFICULTIES OF PADDLING THROUGH THE ICE FLOES, THIS IS A POPULAR DESTINATION FOR SEA KAYAKERS.
below THE TEMPERATE CLIMATE AND BEAUTIFUL SCENERY MAKE KAYAKING IN ST PAUL'S BAY, LINDOS ON RHODES IN THE GREEK ISLANDS A HIGHLY PLEASURABLE AND RELAXING EXPERIENCE. THE INTERESTING HISTORY OF THE AREA ALSO MAKES FOR INTERESTING INLAND HIKES.

Scandinavia and Greenland

Greenland and the Scandinavian countries are surrounded by the Atlantic Ocean. Sea kayaking has its origins in Greenland, and its popularity as a recreational activity here and throughout Scandinavia can be ascribed to a relatively mild coastal climate during the summer months, offering a mixture of good paddling and wilderness experiences.

Western Europe

Sea kayaking is well organized in the UK, where the modern sport of sea kayaking began in the 1960's, and some of the more popular spots include northern and southwest Wales, where relatively calm waters lap dramatic coasts, and the west coast of Scotland, which is dotted with islands that offer exciting paddling.

Ireland's irregular eastern coastline and its many islands, bays, undulating hills and lakes support an active sea kayaking fraternity.

A strong kayaking following exists in Germany, whose coastline, in addition to the North Sea on the northwest, includes the Baltic Sea to the northeast. Portugal, France and Spain offer a diversity of sea kayaking conditions in the Atlantic Ocean to the west. The true Mediterranean countries of Italy and Greece, surrounded by over 200 islands set in the Ionian, Adriatic and Aegean seas, are, not surprisingly, popular sea kayaking destinations.

Asia

Rafting and kayaking have become popular activities in Japan, its four principal islands and 3000 small islands bordering the mighty Pacific Ocean to the east – as well as in neighbouring Taiwan.

Lying to the southwest, in the Indian Ocean, is the Maldives archipelago, whose 1190 small islands (only 202 of which are inhabited) are popular among sea kayakers holidaying at the multiple hotels established on the islands.

Sea kayaking is well established around the tropical islands of southern Thailand, which offer some of the world's most navigable waters. Phang Nga Bay, north of Phuket, offers 400km² (155 sq miles) of calm waters across which are scattered 40 limestone islands featuring their unique hongs, collapsed caves with vertical walls reaching to the sky.

above SEA KAYAKERS HAVE ACCESS TO MANY OF THE MOST BEAUTIFUL SITES IN THE WORLD, SUCH AS ROCK ISLAND, PALAU, WITH ITS STUNNING CLEAR BLUE WATERS AND ROCK FORMATIONS.
below SEA KAYAKING IS VERY POPULAR IN THE UK. HERE, SEA KAYAKERS EXPLORE THE BASE OF THE STRIKING LIMESTONE CLIFFS OF WHITESHEET ROCK, LYDSTEP POINT, IN PEMBROKESHIRE, SOUTH WALES.

Southern Africa

Along the east coast of Southern Africa, Malawi's Lake Nyasa (Lake Malawi) separates that country from Mozambique — both excellent kayaking destinations. Lake Nyasa, taking up a fifth of the country, has a mainly subtropical climate. Sea kayak touring on the massive lake brings paddlers in contact with Africa's wilderness, traditional villages, ancient dugout canoe paddlers, and a magnificent freshwater underwater world. Mozambique's tropical coasts are still in a virtually pristine state, with coral reefs and lagoons fringing the Indian Ocean coastline. Sea kayaking around Inhambane and the Bazaruto Archipelago in central Mozambique is outstanding.

Namibia offers sea kayaking routes along the Skeleton Coast, with the focal point being Walvis Bay (chief port and fishing centre).

Well-established in South Africa, sea kayaking routes start with the cold waters of the Atlantic Ocean on the arid but unspoiled west coast, and move to the protected waters of the Cape Peninsula. The south and east coasts offer the warm waters of the Indian Ocean, from the Garden Route, with its indigenous forests stretching down to the shore, to the rugged Wild Coast and ending at the St Lucia Wetlands, one of Africa's largest estuaries, and a World Heritage Site.

Australia and Oceania

Classic Australian sea kayaking spots include the Sydney Harbour area, fed by the Tasman Sea on Australia's east coast; the Great Barrier Reef area south of Cairns and around the Whitsunday Islands; and South Australia off Adelaide. Perth, on the west coast, also has fine routes, made more attractive by the gentle climate and warm water.

New Zealand has a long history of sea kayaking, as the original Polynesian settlers arrived there by sea

TONDONI BEACH, PEMBA ISLAND, ZANZIBAR, IN TANZANIA, LURES SEA KAYAKERS WITH WARM WATERS TYPICAL OF THE TROPICS.

above THE HUNDREDS OF KILOMETRES OF WATERWAYS IN THE ABEL TASMAN NATIONAL PARK ON THE NORTHWESTERN TIP OF THE SOUTH ISLAND, NEW ZEALAND, PROVIDE MANY DAYS OF PADDLING THROUGH BEAUTIFUL SCENERY IN A RELATIVELY MILD AND TRANQUIL CLIMATE.

below SEA KAYAKING IN A RELATIVELY PROTECTED AREA, SUCH AS A BAY OR HARBOUR, IS A REAL PLEASURE IN TEMPERATE CLIMATES. HERE A KAYAK HEADS TOWARDS TA'AROA HEAD, IN OTAGO HARBOUR, NEW ZEALAND.

canoe. The coastlines are punctuated with multiple inlets and fjords (especially on the South Island), which are superb for sea paddling. The Abel Tasman National Park and the Marlborough Sounds on South Island offer hundreds of kilometres of sheltered waterways, which comprise some of the most stunning and tranquil sea-kayak touring areas to be found.

The islands of Oceania, in the Pacific Ocean, include some of the world's most exotic destinations. They encompass Vanuatu, Fiji, Papua New Guinea, the Solomon Islands, and Palau, as well as Guam, the islands of Micronesia, the Marshall Islands, Tuvalu, Samoa, and Tonga. Oceania has always been associated with images of a tropical paradise, attracting sea kayakers who have an insatiable wanderlust and a romantic sense of adventure.

Directory of website addresses

Australia
Maatsuyker Canoe Club
(Tasmania) at
www.tassie.net.au/~lford/
New South Wales Sea Kayak Club
at www.seakayak.asm.au/
Queensland Canoeing at
www.squirrel.com.au/business/
qldcanoe/
Amateur Canoe Association of
Western Australia at
www.iinet.net.au/~rokhor/cano/
index.html

Canada
Canadian Recreational Canoeing
Association (CRCA) at
www.crca.ca/index.html
Great Lakes Sea Kayaking
Association at
www.geocities.com/Yosemite/
Gorge/4657/

Central America
Baja Expeditions (Mexico) at
www.bajaex.com
Gulf Island Kayaking (Caribbean
Islands) at
www.islandnet.com/tour
Wildways Caribbean Adventure
Travel (Trinidad and Tobago): Pan
Caribe Tours, PO Box 3223 Austin,
TX 78764

Finland
Espoon Eskimot r.y. at
www.megalos.fi/~eses/
Helsingin Melojat at
www.helsinki.fi/~alind/
Heme1.htm

Iceland
The Icelandic Kayak Club at
www.centrum.is/kayak/enska

Germany
German Canoe Union at
www.kanu.de
Salzwasser-Union at
www.salzwasserunion.de

Ireland
ISKA www.iol.ie/~dwalco/

Madagascar/ Indian Ocean Islands
Real Cape Adventures at
www.seakayak.co.za

Mozambique
Real Cape Adventures at
www.seakayak.co.za

New Zealand
New Zealand Canoeing
Association at
www.actrix.gen.nz/users/
msavory/nzca.htm

Norway
Norwegian Canoe Association
www.padling.no/nindex.html

South Africa
Recreational & Commercial Sea
Kayaking Association of South
Africa (RECSKASA) at
www.recskasa.org.za
Canoeing South Africa at
www.canoesa.org.za

South America
Patagonia Altue Expedciones
Patagonian Kayak
e-mail: altue@entelchile.net

Tanzania
Coastal Kayaking Trails at
www.kayak.co.za

Thailand
Sea Canoe at www.seacanoe.com

UK
Jersey Canoe Club at
www.jcc.org.je/
British Canoe Union at
www.bcu.org.uk, also has
links to many UK clubs

USA
American Canoe Association at
www.aca-paddler.org
Trade Association of Sea Kayaking
(TASK) at
www.viewit.com/wtr/TASK.html
Californian Kayak Friends at
www.ckf.org
Gulf Area Sea Paddlers (Florida)
at www.gasp-seakayak.org/
San Francisco Bay Area Sea
Kayaking Kayakers (BASK) at
www.bask.org
e-mail: bask@bask.org
Trade Association of Paddle
Sports (TAPS) at
www.gopaddle.org

Glossary

anemometer: instrument which measures wind speed, indicating whether it is safe to go out in a kayak

barometer: mechanical or digital instrument which reads atmospheric pressure, allowing the paddler to predict changes in the weather

bilge pump: various types of pumps are available for effective removal of water from the kayak

brace/bracing: to place or sweep the paddle in the water at the correct angle to stabilize or turn the kayak

broach/broaching: when the kayak turns parallel to a wave

clapotis: incoming swells colliding with water falling back from a barrier such as a sea wall or cliff

dry suit: loose-fitting suits with waterproof latex seals and waterproof zippers. They keep the paddler dry and markedly increase survival time in cold seas. Usually worn with warm undergarments in colder climates

feathered paddle: paddle with blades set at an angle of up to 90 degrees to one another

paddle float: inflatable float which fits over the blade of a paddle, used during paddle float rescue/re-entry

paddle float re-entry: rescue technique in which paddle float is fitted and paddle is placed across rear of kayak, thereby creating an effective outrigger to assist the paddler in re-entry

paddle shaft/loom: mid-section of paddle, pole with paddle blades at either end

paddle park: device on the rear of the kayak, just behind the cockpit, into which a paddle may be fitted during a paddle float rescue. Holds paddle in place

perling: when the kayak buries its nose in the trough of a wave and the paddler tips forward out of the craft

PFD (Personal Flotation Device): flotation jacket, required safety wear for kayakers

pogies: neoprene/nylon mittens designed to cover only the top of the closed fist, protecting the hands while allowing a bare-handed grip on the paddle shaft

power face/driving face: the flat or slightly concave surface of the paddle blade

roll/rolling: recovery technique used after a capsize (various rolling techniques are discussed in Chapter 3)

sea anchor/drogue: a small parachute that fills with water when deployed from the bow of the kayak; creates resistance to slow the downwind drift of a kayak

spraydeck: watertight cockpit cover which protects a larger area than the sprayskirt

sprayskirt: skirt fitted with shoulder straps, which is worn by the paddler and attaches to the cockpit rim of a sit-in kayak

unfeathered paddle: paddle with blades set on one plane

wet exit: falling out of the kayak into the water

wet suit: suit or item (shorts, jacket etc) which protects the paddler by allowing a thin layer of water inside, which is warmed by the body and insulates the paddler from cold water outside

PHOTOGRAPHIC CREDITS

African River Craft: pp19 (bottom right); **Michael Aw:** p91 (top); **Andy Belcher:** pp 54, 71, 82; **Roger de la Harpe:** 76, 92; **Roy Dumble:** pp36, 73, 88 (bottom); **Easy Rider:** p19 (bottom left); **Gallo Images:** p49; **Bill Hatcher:** pp 9, 18 (bottom left), 35 (top), 42, 72, 77, 80, 84, 89; **Johan Loots:** p60; **Michael McCoy:** pp6, 18 (bottom right), 75, 86, 75, 88 (top); **Minnesota Tourism:** pp5, 8; **Mountain Camera/John Cleare:** pp61, 63, 85, 91 (bottom); **Mountain Camera/Rupert Grey:** p90 (top); **Mountain Camera/Colin Monteath:** pp27, 79, 93 (top); **National Library:** p11; **Photo Access/Getaway/C. Lanz:** pp 13,21; **PhotoBank/Peter Baker:** p91 (bottom); **Prijon Gmb:** pp 29 (top), 32 (top & bottom), 87 (top left & top right); **David Rogers:** pp12, 24, 41, 47, 64, 76; **David Wall:** pp2, 10, 40, 46, 58, 81, 93 (bottom).

Index

BIBLIOGRAPHY

Dowd, J Sea Kayaking: a Manual for Long-distance Touring. Vancouver: Greystone Books, 1997

Ferrero, Franco Sea Kayak Navigation. Great Britain: Pesda Press, 1999

Ford, K Whitewater and Sea Kayaking, Outdoor Pursuit Series. Windsor: Human Kinetics Publishers Inc, 1995

Foster, N Sea Kayaking. Fernhurst Books, 1991

Guillion, L Canoeing and Kayaking Instruction Manual. Newington, VA: American Canoe Association, 1987

Hanson, J Complete Sea Kayak Touring. Camden, Maine: Ragged Mountain Press, 1998

Harrison, D Kayak Touring (Ed). Mechanicsburg, PA: Stackpole Books, 1998

Hutchinson, D C Guide to Expedition Kayaking on Sea and Open Water. Third Edition. Old Satbrook, Connecticut: The Globe Pequot Press, 1995

Johnson, S Sea Kayaking: Woman's Guide. Camden Maine: Ragged Mountain Press, 1998

Kellog, Z The Whole Paddler's Catalog (Ed). Camden, Maine: Ragged Mountain Press, 1997

Loots, J A Practical Guide to Sea Kayaking in Southern Africa. Cape Town: Struik Publishers, 1999

Seidman, D The Essential Sea Kayaker: A Complete Course for the Open Water Paddler. Camden, Maine: Ragged Mountain Press